GLORY DAYS

STEAM IN EAST ANGLIA

PETER SWINGER

AMBERLEY

First published 1999, this edition 2020

Amberley Publishing
The Hill, Stroud
Gloucestershire, GL5 4EP

www.amberley-books.com

British Library Cataloguing in Publication Data.
A catalogue record for this book is available from the British Library.

ISBN 978 1 4456 9964 6 (print)
ISBN 978 1 4456 9965 3 (ebook)

Typeset in 10pt on 13pt Sabon.
Typesetting by Aura Technology and Software Services, India.
Printed in the UK.

Contents

Introduction

Whilst I was born deep in Great Western Railway territory in Cardiff, my real introduction to the glory of steam came on the East Suffolk main line of what had been the Great Eastern Railway. I deeply regret not being able to remember the things which I must have witnessed at Cardiff General and on the lines along the South Wales coast in my early childhood for there must have been 'Saints' and 'Stars' and much more that has long gone to the cutter's torch.

The vagaries of war brought the family to Suffolk in 1944 or 1945 and, at the age of about thirteen, a family move necessitated my travelling to school daily from Darsham to Woodbridge. This meant my catching a train from the former station at somewhere around 7.30 a.m. and resulted in my arriving at school at about 8.15; the time on the train and the early arrival at school (in theory!) gave me time to finish the homework or 'prep' as it was known. The train home in the afternoons left Woodbridge at 3.42 p.m. and, as school lasted until 3.30 p.m., I had permission to leave five minutes early each day. However, I regularly had to remind the masters of this fact, as a result of which the train became known as 'The Darsham Flyer' – perhaps I should have had a headboard made. Sometimes it resulted in 'prep' not being set for the night leading to a certain popularity with my classmates.

The morning motive power was most frequently a 'B17', usually either No. 61664 *Liverpool* or No. 61665 *Leicester City*; the latter was the subject of my very first railway photograph – and truly awful it was. 'B12s' and 'D16s' also featured prominently and *Claud Hamilton* itself was a regular performer but the 'Britannia' Pacifics never worked anything as mundane as my school trains nor yet the daily workings on the East Suffolk main line, although they did eventually become regular motive power on the 'Easterling'.

The morning train from Darsham was almost always brought up at the rear by an articulated pair of carriages of open design, the origin of which I have never been able to establish. However, they were certainly of Gresley design and I never did discover by which return working they got back to Yarmouth ready for the next morning. They just may have been from the 'East Anglian' set built in the late 1930s.

The acquisition of my first Ian Allan 'abc' of Eastern Region locomotives came quite soon after the move and the rest, as the saying goes, is history, for the bug had bitten. It was joined a few years later by an abiding passion for motor racing. As the years have rolled on, I have been surprised to find just how many people have these twin interests.

One evening on Ipswich station, I was invited on to the footplate of *Britannia*. For some reason the locomotive was uncoupled and moved forward and back to recouple. It was my first time on a locomotive in steam (or in any other condition for that matter) and that overawed youth little thought that one day he would be part owner of the leviathan upon which he stood but such would be the decree of destiny.

Following National Service, the interest in railways waned as the urge, nay – the necessity – of racing cars took precedence. I regret missing the passing of steam for it would have been perfectly feasible to cover both activities, but the earlier bug returned one day when *Flying Scotsman* worked a special into Norwich past Snetterton where we were competing. The day's schedule allowed us to practise, photograph the passing of the train (the line passes less than a mile from the circuit), race, take the Lotus home and then return to photograph No. 4472 on its return passage through Thetford.

Apart from the Pacifics preservation has not been kind to the London & North Eastern Railway and its forebears for there are precious few locomotives left. It is a tragedy that no 'B17' and no 'Claud' was saved – no doubt this was due to nearly all of them having gone to the cutters before the preservation movement really took off but it is a relief that two of Thompson's 'B1s' have been preserved.

My previous book, *On Great Eastern Lines*, has, apparently, been a resounding success and the sales department at Ian Allan Publishing wants another book on East Anglia. It is, therefore, with gratitude and humility that I offer you *Glory Days: Steam in East Anglia*. I hope you enjoy it as much as I have enjoyed putting it together.

Peter Swinger
Stowmarket

This is Brentwood Bank in 1901 with GER Class D16 No. 1883 at the head of an Up Cromer express. The stainless steel ring on the smokebox door is seen to good effect as are the large spectacles on the cab front. Compare this picture with the situation nearly a century later with the tracks expanded to four and the area entirely built up. (L&GRP)

The 'Tilbury Universal Machines' made their appearance in 1880. No. 40 *Black Horse Road* was built in 1807 by Sharp, Stewart and is seen near Southend at the head of an Up passenger working bound for Fenchurch Street on an unknown date. Under Midland Railway ownership, the locomotive became No. 2149, later becoming No. 2138 when it passed to the LMSR. The train appears to consist entirely of four-wheelers. The company crest is carried upon a plaque on the tank-side with the name in a semicircle around it whilst the small white plate atop the smokebox proclaims 'LTSR'. (L&GRP)

Background

There are sometimes conflicting ideas as to which parts of England comprise East Anglia: within these pages are to be described and illustrated the steam trains which ran within the counties of Essex, Suffolk, Norfolk and parts of Cambridgeshire. Moreover, the book concentrates upon the years between the mid-1930s and the end of steam with reference to earlier days for nothing can be seen in total isolation.

From the time of its incorporation under the Great Eastern Railways Act of 7 August 1862 from a considerable number of smaller companies, the Great Eastern Railway held sway throughout East Anglia with niggling incursions from other railway companies in Norfolk and Essex. In north Norfolk the Midland & Great Northern Joint Railway had its line running from Bourne to Norwich, Cromer and Great Yarmouth whilst, in the south of Essex, the London, Tilbury & Southend Railway spoiled the Great Eastern's monopoly.

A lot of Cambridgeshire was Great Eastern territory. However, the Great Northern Railway's East Coast main line ran through the western area of that county and the London & North Western Railway (of all people!) obtained a foothold in East Anglia by virtue of its route from Oxford and Bletchley to Cambridge, and there was an encounter with the Great Northern with its branch from Hitchin. At the Grouping in 1923 all that had been Great Eastern territory passed to the London & North Eastern Railway, but the Midland & Great Northern Railway existed as a separate entity until 1 October 1936 when working was taken over by the London & North Eastern Railway.

In the heart of Suffolk lay the Mid-Suffolk Light Railway which escaped the clutches of the LNER (probably because that company really did not want it!) and it remained independent for a further quarter of a century. This little rural byway was said to start from nowhere (Haughley) and finish in the middle of a field (Laxfield). And on the Suffolk Coast was the wondrously incongruous Southwold Railway, which would, undoubtedly, have been preserved in its entirety had it managed to survive for but a few years more. It was the only 3 ft gauge railway in East Anglia and finally closed in 1929.

The London, Tilbury & Southend Railway opened in July 1854 to start a somewhat chequered fifty-year-long career, thirty-seven of which would be entirely independent, but that independence came to an end on 7 August 1912 when the company was taken over by the Midland Railway (in the face of strong opposition from the Great Eastern Railway which was eventually withdrawn) with the result that at the Grouping the London, Midland & Scottish Railway (the largest of the 'Big Four') had a tentacle in East Anglia.

Ownership of the railways of mainland Great Britain from 1 January 1948 passed to the State and all of the main line railways in East Anglia passed to British Railways, including the Mid-Suffolk: it was under British Railways that the Midland & Great Northern finally ceased to be, virtually all evidence that it had ever existed being wiped from the map of East Anglia before the Beeching axe.

All railways must start from somewhere and whilst they are not in East Anglia mention must be made of the four London termini from which the railways of East Anglia emanated. At the time of the creation of the Great Eastern Railway the London terminus of the Eastern Counties Railway was at Shoreditch, but this station soon proved to be inadequate and the directors of the new Company decided to build their new terminus at Liverpool Street, opening it on 2 February 1874. The station was in something of a dip, being below the surrounding street level, necessitating a considerable climb out and up to Bethnal Green, not to mention the destruction of a not inconsiderable number of dwellings.

The London, Tilbury & Southend Railway had been promoted jointly by the Eastern Counties Railway and the London & Blackwall Railway so it is not too surprising to find that it was from Bishopsgate and Fenchurch Street that the first trains ran on 13 April 1854, the lines joining at Stratford and thence running to Tilbury and Southend. From King's Cross a line ran to Cambridge.

Having made the steep climb to Bethnal Green the lines of the Great Eastern Railway divided, the one turning to the left and northwards heading for Cambridge and Norfolk and the other to the right and eastwards to Essex, Suffolk and Norfolk. The Cambridge-bound line passed through Bishops Stortford and Elsenham, passing into Cambridgeshire and on through Audley End (with its twin tunnels so that the local land owner would not be offended by the sight of trains over his land!), Whittlesford and Shelford before gaining the Varsity City and meeting the line from Haughley coming in from Bury St Edmunds and Newmarket. North of Cambridge lay Barnwell Junction with branches to St Ives and Mildenhall and continuing to Ely, north of which lay a major junction with lines running west, north and east. From this junction the westward line ran to March (another important junction) and Peterborough which was the furthest west that the Great Eastern Railway ever extended. The northbound line from Ely ran through Littleport to Denver (junction for Stoke Ferry and the privately owned Wissington Light Railway) and on to Magdalan Road where it met the line from the junction at March: approximately halfway along that section of line lay the Wisbech & Upwell Tramway which ran beside the road for most of its length, necessitating the use of tram engines with cow-catchers and skirted motion. Continuing northwards the line attained King's Lynn and Hunstanton with a junction at Meacham which took the railway to Wells-next-the-Sea. The easterly line from Ely went to Norwich via Thetford and Attleborough and eventually to Great Yarmouth.

Returning to Bethnal Green the eastbound line led to Essex, Suffolk and Norfolk. Some four miles out from Bethnal Green lay Stratford, the site of the locomotive works of the Great Eastern Railway where a world record for the construction of a steam locomotive was set which still stands: on 10 and 11 December 1891 a 'Y14' class 0-6-0 steam locomotive was erected in 9 hours 37 minutes. Ahead from Stratford lay Shenfield (the junction for the line to Southend) and Chelmsford (the county town of Essex) and Witham which was a junction for Braintree and Dunmow and a connection with the Cambridge line at Bishop's Stortford.

Further on, at Kelvedon, was the junction for the Kelvedon & Tollesbury Light Railway, whilst at Marks Tey a further line struck northwards to Long Melford where it split with routes going west and east: the former representing the Colchester–Cambridge cross-country route whilst the latter went to Bury St Edmunds. At Bury, it joined the Ipswich–Cambridge main line.

After Marks Tey came Colchester with its junction for Brightlingsea, Walton-on-the-Naze and Clacton-on-Sea. At one time there was a British Railways sign at the booking hall at Colchester which bore the legend 'Harwich for the Continent' to which some worthy had added 'Frinton for the Incontinent' but, sadly, it disappeared.

The locomotive history of the railways of East Anglia is, to say the least, diverse. From its opening the London, Tilbury & Southend Railway was leased to the contractor who had built it at a guaranteed return of 6 per cent on the capital of £400,000 plus half the profits – but there never were any of those. Whilst leased the railway never owned any rolling stock or locomotives (is history repeating itself under privatisation?), neither was it properly signalled and when the lease expired on 3 July 1875, the directors came to an agreement whereby the Great Eastern Railway would continue to supply the locomotives for five years and the rolling stock for two years. This agreement came to an end in January 1880 by which time the London, Tilbury & Southend Railway had built some locomotives for itself.

The Midland & Great Northern Joint Railway was created in July 1893 by the Midland and the Great Northern railways, which took over the Eastern & Midlands Railway. This railway had been created on 1 January 1883 by the amalgamation of the Lynn & Fakenham Railway, the Yarmouth & Norfolk Railway and the Yarmouth Union Railway. Six years, to the day, later the Eastern & Midlands Railway absorbed the Midlands & Eastern Railway which had itself been constituted on 27 March 1866 from the amalgamation of the Norwich & Spalding Railway, the Spalding & Bourne Railway and the Lynn & Sutton Bridge Railway. The Peterborough, Wisbech & Sutton Bridge Railway contrived to remain independent front the Midlands & Eastern but came into the Eastern & Midlands fold in 1883. The resultant locomotive stock inherited by the Midland & Great Northern Joint Railway was, therefore, bewildering in its complexity. The locomotive works of the Midland & Great Northern was created at Melton Constable – a veritable Crewe in deepest rural Norfolk.

The Great Eastern Railway inherited a motley collection of locomotives from its constituent railway companies and a wide variety continued to be built at Stratford, for the locomotive works became something of a nursery for locomotive superintendents as they came and went to other railway companies – no doubt attracted by higher emoluments than the Great Eastern was able to afford!

Under the LNER the Gresley influence had its impact on the railways of East Anglia, his only class of 4-6-0 being initially specifically built to cope with increasing loads on the Great Eastern section. Similarly, his successor Edward Thompson left his mark but the final flowering of steam power in the area came following Nationalisation.

Robert Riddles CBE was the first Chief Mechanical & Electrical Engineer of British Railways and it was under his guidance that the Class 7MT Pacifics were produced, the first fifteen of them being allocated initially to Stratford and Norwich.

East Anglia was the first area of England to see steam eradicated from its train services under the 'Modernisation' programme and this most evocative form of railway traction was gone by the early 1960s.

Ex-London & North Western Railway Class 1P 2-4-2T No. 6708 is pictured at the head of the 2.7 p.m. Cambridge–Bletchley train on 19 January 1935. These engines had been built to a design of Webb between 1890 and 1897. They were provided with 5 ft 6 in. driving wheels and boilers pressed to 150 psi. They had 17 in. x 24 in. cylinders and weighed 50.5 tons. A total of 160 of the class were built, with no less than 157 passing to the LMS and forty-three surviving to see Nationalisation. Cambridge is a strange station operating on one extremely long platform and four bay platforms. It was the deepest incursion the LNWR made eastwards. (Author's collection)

Early Steam

Whilst the intention of this volume is to concentrate on the period which can be regarded as the Glory Days of steam in East Anglia from the mid-1930s to the end of steam working in the area in the early 1960s, nothing can be seen in total isolation so it is appropriate to take a brief look at what preceded the main subject.

As noted already, upon its incorporation in 1862 from a considerable number of smaller companies the Great Eastern Railway inherited a motley and varied collection of locomotives, though it was not unique in suffering this encumbrance.

Robert C. Sinclair had come to the Eastern Counties Railway from the Caledonian Railway in 1856 and was in charge at Stratford upon the formation of the Great Eastern Railway, remaining in office until 1866 and leaving a decided mark upon the locomotive history of the Company. It was under Sinclair that something approaching a standard design made its appearance in the form of his 'Y' class 2-4-0s, no less than 110 of which were built commencing in 1859, construction continuing until the year of his retirement. Strange to relate, none of them were built at Stratford: Neilson & Co. built the first twenty, Robert Stephenson & Co. and R. & H. Hawthorn were responsible for fifteen each, whilst Kitson & Co. and the Vulcan Foundry were each responsible for twenty-five. For the final batch of ten the GER went across the Channel to the French firm of Schneider et Cie of Le Creusot. These well-proportioned engines had 17 in. by 24 in. cylinders, 6 ft 1 in. driving wheels, with boilers pressed to 120 psi. Depending upon the builder they weighed from 30 to 33 tons or 51.75 to 54.75 tons with the tender: their numbers ran consecutively from 307 to 416 inclusive.

Although intended as freight engines the 'Y' class proved so successful that many were drafted to passenger service and twenty of them were rebuilt as 4-4-0s, the last survivors of both wheel arrangements remaining in service until 1894.

Successful though the 'Y' was, Robert Sinclair is best remembered for his 'W' class single-driver 2-2-2, of which thirty-one were built between 1862 and 1867. Once again, the construction of these engines (which were destined to be responsible for the principal expresses for twenty years) was farmed out, none of them being erected at Stratford. Fairburn & Co. built five, Slaughter, Gruning & Co. and Kitson & Co. ten apiece and the French firm of Schneider et Cie was again called upon, building six. The boiler was pressed to 120 psi, feeding its steam to 16 in. by 24 in. cylinders with 7 ft 1 in. driving wheels, the upper part of which was encased in elaborately pierced splashers. Under Robert Sinclair, Great Eastern Railway engines were painted pea green with black boiler bands and red lining.

Upon the retirement of Sinclair, Samuel H. Johnson came to Stratford in July 1866 where he found his new employer short of motive power, with many of the older engines on their last legs – there was an urgent need for new locomotives for both passenger and freight duties. Indeed, so dire was the situation that with the agreement of the North British Railway for which they were being built by Neilson, Reid & Co., five 2-4-0 mixed traffic engines were delivered new to Stratford early in 1867. The GER built three similar engines in 1868 at Stratford. These locomotives formed the prototype of the well-known 'No. 1' class sometimes known as the 'Little Sharpies', forty of which were turned out between 1867 and 1872: thirty came from Sharp, Stewart & Co. and the remainder were built at Stratford. As constructed for the North British Railway the new engines had 6 ft 0.25 in. driving wheels which were reduced to 5 ft 7 in. and the 16 in. by 20 in. cylinders were increased to 16 in. by 22 in: they carried the highest-pressed boilers yet seen on the Great Eastern at 140 psi and turned the scales at 29 tons in working order or 47 tons with the tender. At the time, the London, Tilbury & Southend Railway was still having its motive power supplied by the Great Eastern, which cannot have helped its own problems and a number of 'Little Sharpies' were loaned until 1880 when the smaller company had acquired an adequate locomotive stock of its own.

Johnson next produced an 0-6-0 goods engine, sixty of which were built – twenty by Neilson & Co. in 1867 and 1868 and the balance of forty by the Worcester Engine Co. from 1867 to 1869. All of the Johnson engines had the characteristic outline which he later took with him almost unchanged to the Midland Railway. The 0-6-0s referred to above were designated '417' and were followed in 1871–2 by the '477' class of which Beyer, Peacock & Co. built the first twenty. R. Stephenson & Co. built a further five and Dubs & Co. and Nasmyth, Wilson & Co. each built five in 1872. The Yorkshire Engine Co. built a further fifteen of them in 1873 – of the firms mentioned, four were supplying the Great Eastern Railway for the first time.

The balance of Johnson's work at Stratford was mainly centred around tank engines but in 1874 his final production appeared and was the only engine he designed for the Great Eastern which was suitable for express passenger work. It was a two-cylinder 4-4-0: even in 1874 the use of a leading bogie was unusual and the new class was the first inside-cylinder 4-4-0 built for an English railway and was classified 'C8' They had 6 ft 6 in. driving wheels, 17 in. by 24 in. cylinders, with boilers pressed to 140 psi. Johnson did not fit his new engines with any brakes, reliance having to be placed upon the tender handbrake! Neither did he build any new tenders for them and for years they ran with any oddment of tenders which just happened to be available. Eventually continuous brakes were fitted and the engines saw service all over the system and even occasionally on Royal Trains: the final two finished their careers as station pilots at St Pancras and Liverpool Street in 1897 and 1898 – No. 306 at the Midland station and No. 305 at the Great Eastern terminus.

William Adams began his brief four and a half-year career at Stratford in July 1873: in view of the rapidly expanding London suburban traffic his first design was an 0-4-4T and they were the only locomotives actually built at Stratford under his superintendence. With Class 61 safely under his bell Adams turned his attention to the main line and designed his first 4-4-0 intended for passenger work.

The new engine had two 18 in. by 26 in. outside cylinders with 6 ft 1 in. coupled wheels, with the boiler pressed to 140 psi: the engine weight was 45 tons and with the tender it was 76 tons. Compared to the Spartan insufficiency of the Johnson designs, the Adams engines had a magnificent cab with glass windows. Given the success of his later designs for the London & South Western Railway, the 'Ironclads', as the GER 4-4-0s were dubbed, enjoyed little success in passenger work and for most of its existence the class was relegated to fast freight services.

However, William Adams was to leave his mark on the Great Eastern for he introduced a new wheel arrangement to Great Britain and gave the first member of his new class a name by which the wheel arrangement was to become universally known.

Fifteen of the new locomotives were built in 1878 and 1879 by Neilson & Co. to the 2-6-0 wheel arrangement. They were equipped with driving wheels of 4 ft 10 in. diameter and the 140-psi boiler delivered its steam to two 19 in. by 26 in. cylinders. There was 1,393 sq. ft of heating surface and 17.8 sq. ft of grate and the engine weighed 46.5 tons. At the time of its introduction the Great Moguls of Delhi were much in the public eye, so it is not surprising that in view of the potential exceptional power the new engine was named 'Mogul' – a name which has stuck with the wheel arrangement ever since. The first engine was numbered 527, and the name was painted upon the sandbox on the running plate above the centre pair of driving wheels onto which the outside cylinders drove. These locomotives did not actually appear until Massey Bromley had taken the reins at Stratford.

Sadly, Adams did not achieve an outstanding success with his Mogul, for the boiler, in spite of the immense heating surface, was unable to deliver enough steam to those 19 in. diameter cylinders and the locomotives were very heavy on coal and oil and they spent their all too short working lives on heavy mineral traffic between Peterborough and London. All fifteen of them went to the scrap heap between 1885 and 1887 after a working life of only seven or eight years.

Under William Adams, Great Eastern locomotives were painted plain black with vermilion lining and buffer beams.

Massey Bromley came to Stratford in February 1878 but his tenure in office was even shorter than that of Adams for he resigned in August 1881: he was, perhaps, unique for a Locomotive Superintendent in that he held a Master of Arts degree from Oxford University. Perhaps his greatest decision was that Stratford should take a far greater share of locomotive production in the future for in a little over thirty years it had built no more than eighty locomotives, the rest having been constructed by outside suppliers – which can hardly have been economic.

Bromley was responsible for one outstanding design which was his 4-2-2 tender engines, ten each of which were built by Dubs & Co. and Kitson & Co. in 1879 and 1881/82 before he made his pronouncement on future locomotive production. The new engines had the largest driving wheels seen on a Great Eastern locomotive at 7 ft 6 in. The cylinders were 18 in. by 24 in. and the boiler pressure remained at the familiar Great Eastern 140 psi. Eight of the class were stationed in East Anglia, four at Yarmouth and four at Norwich. They were fully capable of hauling trains at 70 mph and of climbing the Bethnal Green Bank without complaint which was quite remarkable from a locomotive with an adhesion weight of only 15 tons from a total weight of 41.75 tons. With the increasing severity of traffic demands the engines were soon outclassed and they all went to the scrap heap between 1890 and 1893.

Bromley retained the plain black of his predecessor but with bolder red lining.

Following Bromley's resignation referred to above there was an interregnum at Stratford during which the Works Manager Í Gillies was in charge until T. W. Worsdell was appointed to the position of Locomotive Superintendent. Despite Bromley's edict regarding locomotive construction at Stratford, total production over thirty-five years had still not reached more than 160 locomotives. Worsdell therefore laid it down that in future all the Great Eastern Railway's locomotive requirements would be met by Stratford and, apart from a few goods engines urgently needed for the opening of the Great Northern & Great Eastern Joint Railways in 1882, he was true to his word.

His first design was the 'G14' class 2-4-0 with 18 in. by 24 in. cylinders, 7 ft coupled wheels (a Great Eastern standard which would continue for a further thirty years), boiler pressed to 140 psi and a weight of 41.25 tons: Stratford built twenty of them in 1882 and 1883.

This design was followed by some 0-6-0 goods engines of Class Y14 which proved to be extremely successful and with scarcely any alteration remained the standard Great Eastern freight locomotive until the end of the nineteenth century. The cylinders were 17.5 in. by 24 in., the boilers were pressed to 140 psi (almost a standard on the GER) and the coupled wheels were 4 ft 11 in. Between 1883 and 1885 Stratford built fifty and a further nineteen came from Sharp, Stewart & Co: Stratford then continued to build them at the rate of ten a year up to 1913 until they ran to a total of 299 examples. That description may sound just a little tongue-in-cheek for under the London & North Eastern Railway they became Class J15, many of them lasting well into British Railways days. One has been preserved and has a home on the North Norfolk Railway.

Around this time Worsdell introduced a locomotive which looked for all the world like a goods brake van that was on fire. They were his tram engines, built to work between Yarmouth Vauxhall and the Fish Wharf: they weighed only 21 tons, with 3 ft driving wheels and cylinder only 11 in. by 15 in. As they were designed to work through the streets these 0-4-0 locomotives had all their working parts enclosed to meet Board of Trade requirements and they had warning bells and cow-catchers. In later years more were built to work the Ipswich docks and the Wisbech & Upwell Tramway in Cambridgeshire. The six-coupled version broke with Great Eastern tradition in 1903 by having their buffer beams painted light blue instead of vermilion and the younger ones would survive to see nationalisation of the railways.

In May 1885 Worsdell left the Great Eastern after only three and a half years to take up a similar position on the North Eastern Railway at Gateshead. During his short time at Stratford he helped materially to put Great Eastern locomotive stock upon a sound and efficient foundation but will probably be best remembered for the introduction of Royal Blue livery for the locomotives, applied first to freight and tank engines as well as those for passenger duties. With this glorious colour came vermilion lining, buffer beams and coupling rods, gold lettering and cast brass numberplates. The livery was to survive as a distinctive feature on GER motive power until the time of austerity forced upon the railway by World War 1.

Above: In 1901, during GER days, 2-4-0 No. 735 of James Holden's Class T19 pilots an unidentified 'S46' 4-4-0 with a Down Yarmouth express near Brentwood; the train consists entirely of six-wheeled coaches. The 'T19' class was introduced in 1886 and built through to 1897; the locomotives were then rebuilt as 4-4-0s between 1905 and 1908, becoming Class D13. A total of 110 'T19s' were built and sixty were rebuilt; fifty-eight of the latter survived until the Grouping with the first being withdrawn in 1922. The 'S46' was better known as the 'Claud Hamilton', a type that became Classes D14, D15 and D16 under the LNER as a result of various rebuildings. It is interesting to contrast the cabs on these two locomotives, which were introduced only fourteen years apart by the same designer, the 'S46' seeing the light of day in 1900. (L&GRP)

Below: One of Alfred Hill's ubiquitous Class N7 0-6-2Ts (GER Class L) is seen on an Up local approaching Gidea Park with a train of bogie slock. As the locomotive carries its GER number 987 but is lettered LNER, it is likely that this picture dates from 1923 or 1924. (L&GRP)

The Holdens, Father and Son

James Holden came to Stratford in 1885 following the departure of Worsdell to Gateshead. Strangely, Holden had started his career at Gateshead with the North Eastern Railway where his uncle, Edward Fletcher, had been Locomotive Superintendent since the company's formation in 1854. Around 1864 he transferred his services to the Great Western Railway at Swindon whence he came to Stratford.

Upon his arrival at Stratford James Holden found that, out of a total stock of 684 locomotives, the Great Eastern Railway owned just eighteen 0-6-0 shunting tanks. His first major achievement was to completely reorganise Stratford and introduce a high degree of standardisation which brought the Works to a position where it was capable of building new locomotives with an exceptionally high efficiency. With this reorganisation completed, Holden was able to tackle the shortage of shunting engines referred to above and, between 1886 and 1896, no less than 170 0-6-0T locomotives were erected at Stratford Works: a further forty were built between 1899 and 1901 with another twenty in 1904, bringing the total up to 230 during his reign.

Prior to this, in his first year in office Holden introduced no less than four separate classes – 2-4-2Ts, 0-6-0Ts, 0-6-0 freight engines and a new 2-4-0 express locomotive: the latter was No. 710, the prototype of the 'T19' class which was destined to become the mainstay of Great Eastern main line service for many years.

No account of James Holden's tenure at Stratford can omit mention of the world record which was established there in December 1891. In 1888 the London & North Western Railway had erected an 0-6-0 at Crewe Works in 25.5 hours and a few months later that record had been reduced to 16.25 hours by the erection of a locomotive at the Altoona Works of the Pennsylvania Railroad in the United States of America. However, Stratford put these records completely in the shade on the 10th and 11th of the month referred to above.

The parts for one of Worsdell's 'Y14' 0-6-0s had been prepared, machined and laid out in readiness but nothing had been done towards the actual erecting until zero hour was reached, which was 9 a.m. on Thursday 10 December.

Then a team of eighty-five men and boys on the engine and another of fifty-two on the tender set furiously to work. Taking an hour for dinner, work continued until 5.30 p.m. when everyone knocked off for the day. Work recommenced at 6 o'clock (!) the following morning and the tender was completed at 7.40 a.m: at 7.15 a.m. both engine and tender began to receive a coat of workshop grey paint. There was an interval for breakfast from 8.15 to 9 a.m. and the engine was completed at 9.10 a.m. on Friday 11 December. The engine and tender of No. 930 were then coupled, the boiler and tender fitted and the fire laid and the locomotive was in steam by 10 a.m: the usual adjustment of weights took place on the weighbridge and she made her trial trip to Broxbourne and back and was then immediately handed over to the running department. No. 930 then ran 36,000 miles before returning to Works for her final coat of paint: she was destined to have a life of forty-three years and was scrapped in 1935 after covering a total of 1,127,750 miles. Such a labour-intensive feat would not be contemplated in the latter half of the twentieth century as it would be commercially unviable. Under the London & North Eastern Railway the 'Y14s' became the ubiquitous Class J15.

As has been seen, James Holden was responsible for a number of locomotive designs during his tenure at Stratford but of all of them the one which was destined to achieve the greatest fame was his final 4-4-0, the pioneer example of which appeared as the nineteenth century drew to its close. It appeared in 1900 and was so numbered in honour of the turn of the century and was named after the Chairman of the Great Eastern Railway, Lord Claud Hamilton, and it was as such that the class were known until the final one was withdrawn well into British Railways days.

James Holden's predecessors had vacillated between 2-2-2, 4-2-2, 2-4-0 and 4-4-0 tender locomotives for express passenger services but he came down firmly on the side of single axles with side-play rather than a leading or trailing bogie. At his accession to power at Stratford the Great Eastern Railway owned seventy-five bogie single or four-coupled engines but by the end of 1897 this number had dwindled to twelve. Then, following thirteen years when he showed no interest at all in locomotive bogies and when that appendage seemed doomed to extinction on the Great Eastern, in the space of no more than three years he produced 4-2-2 and 4-4-0 passenger engines and an 0-4-4T locomotive for suburban use, the culmination of his work being the 'Claud Hamilton' 4-4-0.

It is sad that colour photography did not exist when *Claud Hamilton* (incidentally, the first and only Great Eastern locomotive to be named apart from *Petrolea* and *Mogul*), for no expense had been spared to beautify the new engine. It carried the dignified Royal Blue livery with scarlet lining out and was embellished with a copper-capped chimney; there was brass beading around the rim of the safety-valve casing, the front and side windows, the capacious cab, the top and bottom of the Westinghouse brake compressor, and the coupled wheel splashers. In contrast with the Royal Blue the buffer beam and coupling rods were vermilion (as had been established by Worsdell) and to top off the whole ensemble a feature of great distinction was introduced which was a broad steel ring, polished bright, encircling the smokebox door and making it possible to dispense with the normal straps across the door. In those days when locomotives really were looked after the overall impression must have been most striking.

The new engine was a simple well-proportioned design with the customary Great Eastern 7 ft driving wheels employing 19 in. diameter by 26 m stroke cylinders. The 4 ft 9 in. diameter parallel boiler was 11 ft 9 in. long, mated to a firebox which was 7 ft long and 4 ft 0.5 in. wide. This provided a total heating surface of 1,630 sq. ft – at the time superheaters were unknown in British locomotive practice. The boiler was pressed to 180 psi and the fire grate was a modest 21.3 sq. ft and this provided a tractive effort of 17,100 lb at 85 per cent of the working pressure, all of which was achieved within a total engine weight of 50 ton 6 cwt. The locomotive was oil fired.

The overall appearance was, perhaps, slightly marred by the tender which Holden chose to couple to his new design: it was a six-wheeler carrying 715 gallons of fuel oil with a ton and a half of coal in a small bunker above the oil tank but the water capacity was very limited at 2,790 gallons; it weighed 35 tons in working order. The top curved inwards instead of the usual outward flare and the whole ensemble had a somewhat 'bunched-up' appearance but this was necessary in order to keep the total wheelbase down to 43 ft 8 in. and so within the compass of a 45 ft turntable. Nevertheless, a century ago the 'Claud Hamilton' was a locomotive of which its designer and owners could well be proud. On the basis of its subsequent performance and longevity, it deserved to rank amongst the most capable 4-4-0 design in British locomotive history.

The choice of the number 1900 came as something of a surprise for, at the time of its construction, numbering of GER locomotives had not advanced beyond No. 1119, but the choice of number was occasioned by the reason given above and by the fact that the locomotive was to be exhibited at the Paris Exhibition of that year. The space for the locomotive's nameplate was achieved by slightly deepening the beading around the leading splasher and thus creating a small panel – somewhat similar to the practice adopted by the London & North Western Railway. After building *Claud Hamilton* there followed a strange process of numbering, subsequent building of members of the class in batches of ten numbered backwards from No. 1900 until Nos 1780–1789 were built in 1923 – the year that the Great Eastern Railway had become merged into the London & North Eastern Railway. The class then totalled 121 examples.

James Holden retired in 1907 to be succeeded at Stratford by his son Stephen Dewar Holden. The appointment of a son in the stead of a brilliant father has occasionally proved to be a success but more often it has proved to be something of an anticlimax – as this change on the Great Eastern Railway proved to be, for the new incumbent stayed but five years before retiring a relatively young man.

As has been seen, construction of the 'Claud Hamilton' 4-4-0 continued through the rest of the independent life of the Great Eastern Railway but increasing train loads on the by no means easy Colchester road had been dictating for some time the requirement of a more powerful engine with greater adhesive weight. The permanent way weight restrictions still imposed a not inconsiderable handicap upon the design staff at Stratford but notwithstanding these restrictions Holden the younger produced his masterpiece in the shape of the 'S69' 4-6-0, the first of which was numbered 1500 and by which number the class was known in Great Eastern and LNER days as 'Fifteen Hundreds'.

The 19 in. by 26 in. cylinders of the 'Clauds' were stepped up to 20 in. by 28 in. and a boiler with its diameter increased to 5 ft 1 in. provided a heating surface increased by 3 sq. ft. This, in itself, would not have been much of an advantage but coupled to a twenty-one-element Schmidt superheater of 286 sq. ft the overall increase in heating area was considerable. However, the main improvement lay in the Belpaire firebox which provided 26.5 sq. ft of grate area compared to 21.3. Thus, with the working pressure remaining at 180 psi the tractive effort rose from 17,100 to 21,970 lb. The original 'Claud Hamilton' had a weight imposition on the coupled wheels of 33 tons; the new engine saw this increased to 43.5 tons – a considerable advance. The weight in working order of No. 1500 was 63 tons.

The appearance of the Great Eastern's first 4-6-0 followed the beautiful lines of the 'Claud Hamilton' including the copper-capped chimney and brass beading to the junction between the smokebox and the boiler barrel, safety valve cover, cab windows (the cab was the most capacious yet fitted to a British locomotive), main splashers and the five pierced apertures in the long secondary splasher extending over the three coupled axles. It was, of course, finished in Royal Blue with vermilion embellishments.

Sadly, the overall impression was marred by the enforced retention of the standard Great Eastern tender, giving the new engine the bunched-up appearance of the 'Claud Hamilton' but its use did serve to keep the overall length down to 48 ft 3 in. and thus within the compass of a 50 ft turntable. The tender accommodated four tons of coal and 3,700 gallons of water.

Construction of the '1500' class continued until 1917, when forty-one had been built. However, no more than forty were in traffic at any one time as No. 1506 was so badly damaged in a collision when working the 'Norfolk Coast Express' at Colchester in July 1913 that she was broken up and never replaced. Under the LNER the '1500s' became the famous Class B12.

It is a great tribute to the design that it was one of the few of which further examples were built well after the formation of the London & North Eastern Railway and Gresley had taken charge as the first Chief Mechanical Engineer. The final batch of 'B12s' were built by Beyer, Peacock & Co. Ltd in 1926 and were numbered 8571–8580, 7000 having been added to ex-Great Eastern locomotive numbers under their new owner.

By the middle of 1954 there were still forty-five of the eighty-one 'B12s' built still at work. During their lives the '1500s' worked as far afield as Aberdeen, Peterhead and Elgin!

Late in GER days, Holden's Class G69 2-4-2T No. 68 passes Gidea Park with a local for Liverpool Street: the coaches in the train had started life as four-wheelers which had later been mounted in pairs on bogie underframes – additionally some had been widened from 8 ft to 9 ft. At the Grouping the LNER classified the class of locomotive 'F6': twenty-two were built – all of them passed to the LNER and two of them survived to see Nationalisation. The first was withdrawn in 1931 and the last in 1948. Because of the amount of glass in the cab they were known as 'Crystal Palaces'. (L&GRP)

Alfred Hill and the Great Eastern Railway

Alfred Hill was appointed to the position of Chief Mechanical Engineer to the Great Eastern Railway at Stratford late in 1912 following the sudden resignation of Steven Holden. Hill was destined to hold the position for ten years until the Great Eastern Railway ceased to exist at the Grouping. Under his guidance Stratford continued to produce Holden junior's 'S69' 4-6-0 for main line passenger work and it was not until 1915 that Hill's first class of locomotive was built.

With the new class, Hill introduced to the Great Eastern a wheel arrangement that was hitherto unknown in East Anglia. With the exception of the 0-6-0 wheel arrangement there had been some not inconsiderable vacillation at Stratford with regard to tank engine policy. Holden senior had abandoned the 0-4-4 favoured by Johnson and Bromley, showing a preference for 2-4-2Ts, then decided to build 0-4-4Ts again in 1898; then in 1911 and 1912 Holden junior reverted to the 2-4-2 wheel arrangement. Hill, however, abandoned both the 0-4-4 and the 2-4-2 wheel arrangement in favour of the 0-6-2T.

Nos 1000 and 1001 were built early in 1915 and fitted with 18 in. by 24 in. cylinders delivering their power to 4 ft 10 in. driving wheels. Until now no locomotive intended for suburban work had been superheated on the GER so, as a comparative test, No. 1001 was superheated and No. 1000 operated on saturated steam: the latter had 1,394 sq. ft of heating surface and the former 1,292 sq. ft. The boiler was pressed to 180 psi and the grate area was 17.7 sq. ft. No 1001 soon demonstrated the advantages of superheating and all later engines of the class were superheated at construction and No. 1000 was soon so equipped. Their weight in working order with 1,600 gallons of water and 3.25 tons of coal was 61.5 tons with an adhesion weight of 49.25 tons – a considerable improvement over the 2-4-2Ts which they were intended to replace. They were equipped with brass-capped chimneys and capacious side-window cabs and thus had a handsome appearance. They were classified 'L77' by Stratford: twelve were built between 1915 and 1921 and a further 110 after the Grouping, Gresley decreeing that the 'N7' (as the class was designated by the London & North Eastern Railway) would become a standard engine for the Great Eastern section. All 122 members of the class passed into BR ownership – a not inconsiderable tribute to Alfred Hill's design. Eight of them survived until 9 September 1962 when steam working ceased south of March. To No. 69685 went the honour of working the final steam-hauled suburban passenger service out of Liverpool Street station on 20 November 1960, when it formed the motive power on the 10.25 p.m. to Hertford East. No. 999 of the class was the last steam locomotive built at Stratford, in March 1924. At the Grouping the locomotive became No. 7999 and then No. 9621 under the 1946 renumbering and this became No. 69621 under BR. No. 69621 was one of the final eight to survive until 1962; following withdrawal, the locomotive was purchased privately for preservation, and now has a permanent home at Chappel & Wakes Colne, headquarters of the East Anglian Railway Museum.

Some would maintain that a locomotive engineer whose main claim to fame was a freight locomotive had not produced anything of any great worth but Alfred Hill's 'magnum opus' was an 0-6-0 tender engine. Soon after his accession to power there emerged from Stratford Works the first superheated version of James Holden's '1150' freight locomotive, Nos 1240–1249. Their appearance suggested a Mogul, for the front overhang was unusually lengthy to allow the front end to accommodate the tail-rods with which the pistons of the inside cylinders were fitted. The engines shared the cylinders of the 'S69'/'B12' at 20 in. diameter by 28 in. stroke and the coupled wheels had a diameter of 4 ft 11 in. – the Great Eastern Railway's standard for freight engines. The boiler was pressed to 160 psi, the grate area was 1,502 sq. ft, the firegrate area was 21.6 sq. ft and the weight in working order 47.25 tons. By lifting the pitch of the boiler centre-line by 7.5 in. above the rail the new engine was given a much more massive appearance than its predecessors. These ten locomotives were GER Class E72 and were classified 'J18' by the LNER at the Grouping.

No more of these engines were built until 1916 but between then and 1920 a further twenty were constructed at Stratford; these were classified 'T77' by the GER and 'J19' by the LNER, which inherited both classes complete at the Grouping. Starting on 1 February 1935 all the 'J18s' were rebuilt to 'J19' specification, the job being completed by January 1938.

The 'magnum opus' referred to earlier was the GER Class D81, which became LNER Class J20. Hill mounted the '1500' boiler pressed to 180 psi on to the 'J18' chassis, thus producing the most powerful 0-6-0 design ever to run on British metals with the sole exception of the Bulleid-designed 'Q1' class of the Southern Railway. The latter boasted a tractive effort of 30,000 lb but exceeded the 29,044 lb of the 'D81' solely by virtue of its boiler pressure of 230 psi. The first 'D81' appeared in 1920 and, by the end of 1922, a total of twenty-five had been built: the enlarged boiler gave a combined heating surface of 1,919 sq. ft which included the 286 sq. ft of the Robinson superheater. The Belpaire firebox served to increase the fire grate area to 26.5 sq. ft, the weight in working order was 54.75 tons and, of course, they retained the 4 ft 11 in. driving wheels. The locomotives were expected to share the fast freight services over the Cambridge main line and for this reason they were vacuum-fitted. They were numbered by the GER 1270–1294 and all passed to the LNER where they were numbered 8270–8294. All became British Railways property. The first was withdrawn in January 1959 and the last in September 1962.

Thus, Alfred Hill left his mark upon the locomotive history of East Anglia.

Ipswich & Bury Railway architecture at its best: this is Bury St Edmunds station in 1874 – the locomotive in view is a 'Little Sharpie'. (Jarman)

This is a truly wondrous example of the motley collection of motive power inherited by the GER at its formation. This 2-4-0T emanated from the Thetford & Watton Railway and was numbered 0802 by its new (and, doubtless, grateful) owner. (L&GRP)

Steam Power on the Tilbury Line

For any railway to introduce two types of locomotive to the country of its origin is no mean feat but for one as small and as short-lived as the London, Tilbury & Southend Railway to do so is quite remarkable – but such was to be its epitaph.

Throughout its life the line had but two men in charge of its locomotives and rolling stock and they carried the unique title of Chief Mechanical & Electrical & Marine Engineer, for the railway was the owner and operator of ships which plied across the Thames. They were the Whiteleggs, father and son.

Thomas Whitelegg came to the London, Tilbury & Southend Railway in 1879. A year later the agreement by which the Great Eastern Railway had supplied the locomotives and rolling stock to work the railway came to an end. However, by then the company had set in motion the means by which it would be able to run its own trains. Starting in 1880, Sharp, Stewart & Co. built a series of Atlantic tanks, the first dozen numbered 1 to 12 were delivered in that year. The design of the 4-4-2Ts has been variously attributed to their builders, to W. Adams (at that time at Stratford with the Great Eastern Railway) and to R. H. Whitelegg: there can be little doubt that the design can be attributed to Whitelegg. These Atlantic tanks were the first of the two locomotive types which the railway introduced to Great Britain and they were to become known as the 'Tilbury Universal Machines' as the railway was eventually to own sixty-nine of them, all of which were named. In fact, with the exception of two 0-6-0s, the Tilbury line named all of its locomotives, including a class of 0-6-2Ts.

The original Atlantic tanks weighed 56 tons and had two 1.7 in. by 26 in. cylinders and 6 ft driving wheels: the first batch had only steam and hand brakes, Westinghouse equipment being added later. As built, they had stovepipe chimneys which, from 1897, were replaced by the handsome Tilbury bell-rimmed chimney. Sharp, Stewart built a further six in 1881 and twelve in 1884. Eight years later, in 1892, Nasmyth, Wilson built Nos 31–36; Sharp, Stewart constructed Nos 37–42 in 1897 and then Dübs was called upon in 1898 to construct Nos 43–48. Nos 49 and 50 were the 0-6-0 tender engines – the only ones the LT&SR ever owned — then in 1900 Sharp, Stewart built Nos 51–62 and North British Locomotive was called upon to build the first of two batches, 63 and 64 in 1902 and 65–68 in 1903. The final 'Tilbury Universal Machines' came from Robert Stephenson in 1909; these were numbered 79–82. Amongst this last batch was the one destined to be preserved – No. 80 *Thundersley* – which currently resides at Bressingham Steam Museum near Diss in Norfolk.

The first batch were known as '1' class: the 1897 batch built by Sharp, Stewart were known as the '37' class (presumably because No. 37 was the first of them). Rapidly increasing traffic had created the requirement for larger engines and the second class of Atlantic tank had 6 ft 6 in. driving wheels, 18 in. by 26 in. cylinders and weighed 63 tons. The Dübs-built examples were also Class 37.

An urgent traffic need in 1899 led to the acquisition of the two 0-6-0s referred to above. They had been built in 1898 by Sharp, Stewart for the Ottoman Railways which had failed to take delivery of them, and they were purchased direct from the manufacturers. They had 18 in. by 24 in. cylinders and 4 ft 6.5 in. driving wheels.

The 1900 and 1903 constructions from Sharp, Stewart and North British Locomotive were '51' class and were dual-fitted for working Midland Railway stock to and from St Pancras and the final four were Class 79. No. 80 was exhibited at the Imperial International Exhibition at the White City in 1909 where it gained a gold medal: whilst on exhibition the locomotive was named *Southend-on-Sea* and received the intended name of *Thunderslev* upon entering service.

In 1903 there appeared the first of Thomas Whitelegg's 0-6-2Ts: they were his first inside-cylindered and six-coupled engines. They were primarily intended for freight traffic: they had 18 in. by 26 in. cylinders, weighed 65 tons and had 5 ft 3 in. coupled wheels. Nos 69–74 were delivered into traffic by the North British Locomotive Co. in 1903, followed by Nos 75–78 in 1908. The final four were built by Beyer, Peacock in 1912 and so did not carry their LT&SR names. This final batch was numbered 2190–2193 by the Midland Railway.

Thomas Whitelegg retired in 1919 – but was to enjoy only a short retirement as he died in 1921 to be succeeded by his son, Robert, who introduced the famous Baltic tanks, the second wheel arrangement to be pioneered in Great Britain by the LT&SR. By Tilbury standards, the Baltic tanks were massive. All eight were built by Beyer, Peacock in 1912 with 6 ft 3 in. coupled driving wheels and 20 in. by 26 in. outside cylinders: as built they employed saturated steam but were later fitted with Schmidt superheaters. They were put into traffic by the Midland Railway which numbered them 2100–2107 and painted standard Midland red. They were renumbered by the LMS in 1929 as Nos 2193–2198, the first and last members of the class having been scrapped in 1929 before receiving their new identities. Nos 2193 and 2194 were also scrapped in 1929 (possibly without receiving their new numbers) and No. 2195 in 1930. No. 2196 went in 1932, No. 2197 in 1933 and the class became extinct in 1934 with the withdrawal of No. 2198.

Through no fault of their own, they were the least successful of the Tilbury locomotives. They were built to work heavy business trains between Fenchurch Street and Southend, but it was only after they were put into traffic that they were found to be too heavy for the bridges west of Barking so could not work into Fenchurch Street.

They were, therefore, employed for a time between Shoeburyness and Southend on through Ealing trains and then between Southend and St Pancras. Finally, they were transferred to the Midland main line where they worked semi-fast suburban trains between St Pancras and Luton.

When increased power was required on the Tilbury line under the London, Midland & Scottish Railway, William Stanier produced a class of three-cylinder 2-6-4Ts and, under British Railways, this wheel arrangement was continued with the BR Standard Class 4MT 2-6-4T engines.

No. 37 *Woodgrange* was also built by Sharp, Stewart as one of the 1897 batch but is distinctly different in appearance, having the cab-roof rounded at its sides. This gives a much more pleasing aspect to the engine. The train is heading for Southend *c.* 1910 and is composed entirely of bogie stock. (L&GRP)

On 3 September 1949 one of J. C. Park's North London Railway Class 2F (as classified by the LMS) 0-6-0Ts No. 27514 was in repose at Devons Road. Built between 1887 and 1905, thirty of these engines were taken into the ownership of the LMSR at the Grouping and fourteen of them survived to become BR property. Devons Road, Plaistow was the principal London locomotive depot of the London, Tilbury & Southend Railway. (R. Harrison)

Above: Still wearing LMS livery on 3 September 1949 Thomas Whitelegg's ex-LTSR Class 37 4-4-2.T No. 2121 was in storage at Devons Road. Sixteen of these handsome locomotives were built between 1897 and 1898 and rebuilt in 1909, all passing to the Midland Railway and eventually to the LMSR. The latter designated them Class 3P and built a further thirty-five examples between 1923 and 1930, all of which passed to British Railways. The first member of the class was withdrawn in 1951 and the last LT&SR-built example was withdrawn in 1952. The class became extinct in traffic in 1960 with the withdrawal of the last LMSR-built example. However, the 'Tilbury Universal Machine' is not completely dead for *Thundersley* is preserved at Bressingham Steam Museum in full London, Tilbury & Southend livery. The engine illustrated here was built in 1925 and was renumbered 41939 by British Railways and on the adjacent road is a Midland Railway Fowler design Class 4P 0-6-0, No. 4332, which was built by the LMSR in 1926. (R. Harrison)

Below: On 3 September 1939 Whitelegg Class 51 4-4-2T No. 2097 was in store at Devons Road. This class was introduced in 1900, twelve being built by Sharp, Stewart and six by North British, all of them passing into LMSR ownership and all lasting to see Nationalisation. Until October 1929 the class was numbered 2158 to 2175, which means that this locomotive would have been LT&SR No. 56 *Harringay*. The class had 6 ft 0 in. driving wheels and a tractive effort of 15,606 lb. No. 2097 was built by Sharp, Stewart (Works No. 4658) in 1900 and was rebuilt in 1924. Although nominally renumbered 41915 at Nationalisation, the locomotive was withdrawn in March 1951 without carrying its new number. (R. Harrison)

Midland & Great Northern Joint Railway

The exact date of this photograph is not known, but this graceful 4-4-0 was built in June 1888 for the Eastern & Midlands Railway, as No. 34, and finished in the company's passenger locomotive livery of brown lined with black and chrome yellow. Then engines had been built initially for the Lynn & Fakenham Railway by Beyer, Peacock as Class A in 1883 at a cost of £3,000 each: they were finished in pale green. The Lynn & Fakenham Railway was amalgamated into the Eastern & Midlands, which became part of the Midland & Great Northern Joint Railway. (L&GRP)

In 1894 Sharp, Stewart & Co. delivered twenty-six 6 ft 6 in. 4-4-0s to the Midland & Great Northern Joint Railway where they became Class C. From 1910 some of them were rebuilt with 'G8' boilers and new cabs: in this later guise No. 38 is seen leaving South Lynn with a Yarmouth train in May 1937. It is wearing the umber livery introduced in 1930. (L&GRP)

The M&GN Class D were 5 ft 2 in. 0-6-0 goods locomotives built in two batches by Neilson & Co. in 1896 and Kitson & Co. in 1898. The type was originally derived from a Midland Railway design, the '2284' class. No. 61 seen here was from the Neilson batch and is pictured in its original form approaching Melton Constable in May 1937. (L&GRP)

LNER Class J3 was Ivatt's Great Northern Railway Cass J4 introduced in 1882: in 1900 Dübs & Co. built twelve of the 5 ft 2 in. engines for the M&GN, which classified them Class DA. In May 1937 No. 084 is seen leaving Spalding with a passenger train for King's Lynn. (L&GRP)

On the last day of February 1959, which was also the last day of operation on the bulk of the ex-Midland & Great Northern Joint Railway, ex-LNER Class J6 0-6-0 (GNR Class J22) No. 64172 leaves South Lynn with the 9.55 a.m. service from Saxby to King's Lynn. (R. Harrison)

This is King's Lynn shed (31C) on 25 September 1958: facing the camera are 'D16/3' 4-4-0 No. 62518 and 'N7' 0-6-2T No. 69620.

On Monday 22 September 1958 ex-LNER Class D16/3 No. 62518 is seen approaching King's Lynn from Hunstanton. The centre road leads to Dereham and Swaffham and that to the right to Ely and Cambridge.

Ex-LMSR Class 4MT Mogul No. 43086 crosses South Lynn 'cut bridge' with the 1.40 p.m. King's Lynn–Peterborough North service for the very last time as it is the last day of February 1959 – the day that the M&GN closed. Note the Great Northern influence in the form of the somersault signal. In Norfolk these engines were nicknamed 'Mangles'; elsewhere on the railways they were known as 'Doodlebugs'.

Potter Heigham station on 27 September 1958 sees ex-LMSR Ivatt Class 4MT Mogul No. 34095 entering the station off the single track whilst an unidentified sister engine waits for the road.

East Anglian Steam under the LNER

Having been Chief Mechanical Engineer with the Great Northern Railway H. N. Gresley was appointed to the same position when the London & North Eastern Railway was formed at the Grouping, the Great Northern being considered the 'senior' of the constituents of the new company. When he authorised the construction of the final batch of 'B12s', Gresley already had in mind the construction of a new class of locomotive to cope with the increasing loads on the Great Eastern Section evinced from the mid-1920s. However, the need for extra motive power was so pressing that the delay in producing a new design could not be allowed to impede the production of some new locomotives; thus the extra 'B12s' were built.

On the surface the provision of a new class of locomotive did not appear to be an insurmountable problem but the restrictions imposed upon the locomotive designers by the civil engineering constraints on the Great Eastern section coupled with the plethora of short turntables, which were still in evidence in East Anglia, dictated that any new locomotive could not be much longer than a 'B12' and produce no greater hammer-blow.

By a long process Gresley decided that the ideal solution would be a three-cylinder 4-6-0 producing around 25,000 lb of tractive effort with a 30 ft grate, a maximum axle load of 17 tons and employing 'D49' cylinders and motion arrangement. It was this specification which the CME sent to Doncaster in 1926: King's Cross drawing office produced at least two drawings – neither of which now exist – whilst Doncaster produced one calling for a taper boiler in order to take some weight off the front end. Sadly, this drawing also did not survive. Initially Doncaster intended having all three cylinders driving on to the leading coupled axle as was found on the ex-North Eastern Railway 4-6-0s. The problem of the axle loading was proving a major stumbling block and eventually Gresley passed it entirely over to the North British Locomotive Co. Ltd which experienced the same difficulties; its first two designs showed axle loads of 18 and 19 tons.

The original specification had called for a locomotive that could run over all Great Eastern main lines, but the Joint Traffic & Locomotive Committee faced up to the inevitable and amended this to 'certain Great Eastern main lines'. As a result, on 17 February 1928, the LNER placed an order with the North British Locomotive Co. for ten locomotives (not twenty as the Locomotive Superintendent required) to be delivered in July and August of that year at a cost of £7,280 each. Doncaster's wish to have the drive entirely on to the leading coupled axle proved impossible and the drive was divided between the leading and centre coupled axles with the middle cylinder placed well forward. The final specification saw an engine with 6 ft 8 in. driving wheels, 17.5 in. by 26 in. cylinders, 27.5 sq. ft of grate, boilers pressed to 200 psi and an overall length of 62 ft 2 in. employing a modified Great Eastern pattern tender. This was Gresley's Class B17 which eventually ran to seventy-three examples spread over five sub-classes. When built they were numbered 2800–2872 and under the 1946 LNER renumbering scheme they became Nos 1600–1672, but because of their original numbering were known to LNER enginemen as 'Twenty-eight Hundreds'.

Whereas the Great Eastern Railway did not have a policy of naming its locomotives the London & North Eastern adopted such a policy with great enthusiasm, naming all of its Pacifics, and the first batch of 'B17s' received the names of stately homes within its territory. With Royal approval the first of them, No. 2800, was named *Sandringham* and it was as 'Sandies' that they became known to enthusiasts.

The 'Sandies' proved very capable machines and were assigned to all the major expresses in East Anglia and in the fullness of time, as more of them were built, they spread throughout the LNER system, the later examples receiving Group Standard tenders. As engineering restrictions were lifted and longer turntables appeared in East Anglia these later examples gravitated to the Great Eastern Section. Capable though they were it is, perhaps, significant that they were outlived by the engines which they had been intended to replace, the 'B12s'.

Gresley is, rightly, best remembered for his Pacifics – the 'A1'/'A3s' and the glorious 'A4s' – but they never worked in East Anglia though they were seen in the Cambridge area. He did, however, produce a class of engine which had a major influence on the Great Eastern Section: it was his 5 ft 2 in. 0-6-0, classified 'J39'. Intended as a freight locomotive these versatile work horses saw considerable service on passenger duties.

During his tenure of office Gresley was responsible for considerable rebuilding of Great Eastern locomotives, extending the lives of the 'B12' and 'D16' classes well into British Railways days.

The CME was knighted in 1936, becoming known as Sir Nigel Gresley and during his time at Doncaster Edward Thompson was put in charge at Stratford. Upon the untimely death in harness of Sir Nigel in 1941 Thompson was promoted to the position of CME to the LNER and proceeded with some alterations to his predecessor's locomotives for which he has yet to be forgiven by railway enthusiasts.

Whilst Thompson's Pacifics were capable but not spectacular machines, he was responsible for two classes which have left their mark on LNER and BR history. Both were classified as mixed traffic locomotives – one of them because it was introduced in wartime. One of these new designs was a 4-6-0 tender locomotive whilst the second was a tank engine of a wheel arrangement – 2-6-4T – that was new to the LNER.

In 1942, whilst hostilities with the little Austrian Corporal were at their height, Edward Thompson's 'B1' class 4-6-0 saw the light of day. Thompson always favoured two cylinders and those on his new engine were 20 in. by 26 in., delivering their power to 6 ft 2 in. driving wheels with steam being delivered from a boiler pressed to 225 psi. The 'B1' produced a tractive effort of 26,880 lb and weighed 123 ton 3 cwt. The initial order was placed in August 1942 with the first ten of the class being numbered 8301–8310. These were finished in apple green. Under the 1946 renumbering scheme, they became Nos 1000 to 1009: the next batch was ordered in May 1944 but the first of them was not built until 1946 so they were numbered in the new series. Darlington Works built the first forty and the first forty-one were named after breeds of antelope or deer; No. 1005 was named *Bongo* and this was just too good an opportunity to miss, so it was by this name that the engines were universally known. The third batch was ordered from North British Locomotive in August 1945 and were put into traffic starting in April 1946 before the Doncaster-built examples. Eventually 410 'Bongos' were built though there were never more than 409 of them in traffic at any one time, as No. 61057 was involved in an accident at Rivenhall End on 7 March 1950 in which it was so badly damaged as to be considered beyond economical repair.

Following the first forty-one, further names were added intermittently over the years, principally after directors and dignitaries of the LNER. The 'B1s' were built well into British Railways days, the last entering service in April 1952. They saw service throughout the LNER system and in British Railways days were found on the Southern and Scottish Regions and were even seen (whisper it low!) at Swindon!

There are those who consider the 'B1' to be the equal of or, perhaps, even better than Stanier's 'Black Five' of the London, Midland & Scottish Railway.

In 1945 Edward Thompson introduced his new tank locomotive which was designated Class L1 and was a 2-6-4 weighing 89 ton 9 cwt: it shared the same cylinder size as the 'B1' and the same boiler pressure but with 5 ft 2 in. driving wheels. The tractive effort was 32,080 lb – not far short of that of the 'A3' Pacifics – and the only tank engines to exceed it were the 'S1' and 'T1' eight-coupled locomotives. A total of 100 'L1s' were built, many of them working in East Anglia and they made the Felixstowe branch their own.

Edward Thompson was succeeded as CME in 1945 by Arthur Peppercorn, who held the position until Nationalisation and then became CME of the Eastern and North Eastern regions of British Railways. The post was abolished in 1949 and Peppercorn retired. He is best remembered for his Pacifics and he was not responsible for the construction of any locomotives specifically designed for use in East Anglia. The final flowering of steam traction on the Great Eastern came under British Railways.

Opposite above: With the Royal Family having a residence within GER territory at Sandringham and the subsequent likelihood of frequent Royal railway travel, from early in the company's history it became the practice to keep one or two locomotive in outstanding condition with the cab roof painted white to work the Royal Train when required. Two Class U16 'Claud Hamilton' 4-4-0s were assigned by Stratford for this duty: on 19 January 1935 No. 8787 could be seen at Cambridge although not on a Royal working. Note the Belpaire boiler and the Westinghouse pump just ahead of the cab. The locomotive looks superb. (Author's collection)

Class E4 2-4-0s were built by the GER from 1891 to 1902 following the designs of James Holden as Class T26. The class ran to 100 examples, all of which passed to the LNER, eighteen of them surviving to see British Railways service. The first to be withdrawn went in 1926 and the last in 1959. In the summer of 1926, No. 7483 is seen leaving Lowestoft with a train of very mixed passenger stock. (Author's collection)

Above: LNER Class F3 had started life as James Holden's Class C32 2-4-2T for the Great Eastern in 1893. The class was built continuously until 1902, eventually running to fifty examples, all of which passed to the LNER, fifteen surviving until Nationalisation. They had 5 ft 8 in. driving wheels, the boiler was pressed to 160 psi and the twin inside cylinders measured 17.5 in. by 24 in. The first of the class was withdrawn in 1936 and the last in 1953. No. 8964 is seen leaving Witham for Braintree with a train of six-wheel non-clerestory stock. (Author's collection)

Below: In April 1928 another member of the class, No. 8067, was to be found waiting to depart from Clacton-on-Sea. (Author's Collection)

The Class B17 4-6-0s underwent some minor but subtle livery changes. As they built, they had 'LNER' and the running number on the tender, the latter later being moved to the cabside and the lettering enlarged upon the tender. Here the second member of the class, No. 2801 *Holkham*, is seen shortly after delivery into traffic near Melton on the East Suffolk main line with a stopping passenger train. The first two coaches are six-wheelers, whilst the remainder of the consist are bogies. (Author's Collection)

Here is a sight never to be repeated. The date is lost, but clearly it comes from the early 1930s. Pictured at Ipswich station, two Class J15 0-6-0s sandwich a 'B17' and a 'B12'. The six-coupled engines are in apple green; the 'B17' is believed to be No. 2827 *Aske Hall*, which is in very clean condition. (Author's collection)

In June 1927 Class B12 4-6-0 No. 8558 departs from Platform 3 at Ipswich with an express for Norwich. The locomotive had been built by William Beardmore of Glasgow in 1920. (Author's collection)

The Class J39 0-6-0 was Gresley's second type of that wheel arrangement designed for the LNER following on from the 'J38s', though both designs appeared in the same year (1926). The 'J39s' had boilers pressed to 180 psi, twin inside cylinders measuring 20 in. by 26 in. and 5 ft 2 in. driving wheels. Intended as freight engines, they often found their way on to passenger duties but, on this occasion, No. 2773 stood on the centre road at Ipswich with an up Norwich cattle train. (Author's collection)

More cattle: on an unknown date in 1935 'J15' 0-6-0 No. 7814 works a mixed cattle and goods train past Melton on the East Suffolk main line. (Author's Collection)

Stephen Holden's Class S69 4-6-0 design for the Great Eastern Railway resulted in a handsome machine, which was probably his magnum opus. However, the attachment of ACFI feed water equipment to some of the class rendered them, well, different. It was felt that they had the appearance of someone with a pack upon his back, which resulted in them earning the nickname 'Hikers'. No. 8500 was the first 'S69' built, as No. 1500; 7000 was added to ex-GER engines at the Grouping and, as No. 8500, the locomotive is seen with ACFI fittings. She looks like an elegant lady in an ill-fitting dress. (L&GRP)

Class B12 4-6-0 No. 8505 enters Ipswich station from the tunnel at the southern end with an express from Liverpool Street in July 1926. The train is pictured running into Platform 4. The locomotive was built in 1913. (Author's Collection)

James Holden's Class T19 2-4-0s were built between 1886 and 1897 and rebuilt as 4-4-0s from 1905 until 1908. Under LNER ownership the type became Class D13. As rebuilt, the locomotives retained their 7 ft 0 in. driving wheels with 180-psi boilers and 18 in. by 24 in. inside cylinders. There were sixty rebuilds, of which fifty-eight passed to the LNER. None, however, survived into British Railways' ownership, the last of the class being withdrawn in 1944. On 23 June 1928, No. 8025 stood at Ipswich station with an empty wagon train. (Author's Collection)

An interesting picture from Platform 3 at Ipswich station in 1931 as Class D14 4-4-0 No. 8880 pilots Class B17/1 4-6-0 No. 2805 *Burnham Thorpe* on a Down express for Norwich. With the passage of time, the locomotive number of the 'B17' has moved from the tender to the cab side and the ownership now appears on the tender in much larger lettering. It is remarkable that this far into the LNER's life, expresses still contained six-wheeled coaches for there is one behind the tender of the 'B17'. In April 1938 the 'B17' was renamed *Lincolnshire Regiment.* (Author's Collection)

Two 'Claud Hamilton' 4-4-0s are pictured double-heading out of Woodbridge with an Up train at 4 p.m. on Saturday 16 June 1928. Class D14 No. 8873 pilots Class D15 No. 8807. (Author's Collection)

Class B17/1 4-6-0 No. 2810 *Honingham Hall* waits to depart from Ipswich with an express. As the train is leaving Platform 4, this indicates that it was bound for Cambridge. It is 1931 and the LNER is still using six-wheeled stock on its expresses as evinced by the coach behind the tender. (Author's Collection)

The LNER made good use of its nearness to the continent, running a not inconsiderable number of boat trains from Liverpool Street to Harwich Parkeston Quay. The company was ever keen on naming its principal expresses, one such being the 'Flushing Continental', which, upon arrival at Parkeston Quay, continued by sea to Flushing in the Netherlands. Here the Down working is seen on Brentwood Bank in 1928 when the motive power, Class B17/1 4-6-0 No. 2803 *Framlingham*, was still very new. On the occasions when the locomotive wore a headboard it was black lettering upon a white background. (Real Photographs)

A stranger far from home – a Great Northern Railway Class H3 Mogul on the East Suffolk main line. No. 4687 is pictured with the 3.30 p.m. ex-Yarmouth slow leaving Woodbridge in September 1920. In 1912 Gresley introduced the first of his Class H2 (LNER Class K1) 2-6-0s and in the following year these were followed by the 'H3' ('K2') class Moguls. The latter carried slightly larger boilers and the former 'K1s' were rebuilt in this form between June 1920 and July 1937. A total of sixty-five original 'H2s' were constructed between 1913 and 1921; of these No. 4687 was one of the last batch of twenty-five constructed by Kitson & Co. in 1920/21. They had 5 ft 8 in. driving wheels, twin 18.5 in. by 26 in. cylinders with boilers pressed to 170 psi. Following the Grouping in 1923, in order to alleviate the motive power problems in East Anglia, Gresley drafted a number of the engines into the area. All the class passed into BR ownership in 1948; the last to be withdrawn succumbed in 1962. (Author's Collection)

Above: The LNER was always in favour of publicity, holding exhibitions at various locations around its territory at regular intervals. One such exhibition was staged at Ipswich in April 1932 and the principal exhibit was the unique Class W1 4-6-2-2 No. 10000. The experimental locomotive is seen entering Ipswich station prior to the exhibition. The white painted hoarding is a signal sighting board but a one-time sales manager to the author, ever in pursuit of advertising sites, thought that it would do very nicely as an advertising hoarding. As built in late 1929, No. 10000 was fitted with a high pressure boiler – pressed to 450 psi – in a four-cylinder compound. Two high pressure 12 in. by 26 in. cylinders drove the leading coupled wheels and two low pressure 20 in. by 26 in. cylinders drove the centre coupled wheels. The locomotive's performance was not up to expectations, with the result that it was stored and, in 1937, rebuilt as a conventional three-cylinder locomotive with streamlining similar to the contemporary 'A4' class. As rebuilt, No. 10000 became No. 60700 under BR ownership. It was to be withdrawn in June 1959 and subsequently scrapped. (R. G. Pratt)

Below: A rare sight in East Anglia: a Gresley Class A3 Pacific is pictured at the head of a Pullman train. No. 2546 *Donovan* is seen at Goldhams Common Curve, Cambridge, on a Down King's Cross–Newmarket Race Special in 1930. (Author's collection)

Above: Starting in 1945, Edward Thompson rebuilt some Gresley 'B17s' as two-cylinder engines with 100A boilers and coupled them to a variety of redundant ex-North Eastern Railway tenders. Just one of them was rebuilt with a 'Group Standard' tender, but the locomotive had been coupled to it from new when built as a 'B17/4' by Robert Stephenson & Co. (No. 2871 as Works No. 4133). The new engine was named *Manchester City* on 11 June 1937: in August 1945 it had the distinction of being the first 'B2' rebuild, as Thompson's design was designated. February 1946 saw the first change of identity – to No. 1671 – and just two months later the locomotive received the accolade of being chosen as the Stratford royal engine and was renamed *Royal Sovereign*. Thereafter No. 1671 was always kept in immaculate condition. In its new guise *Royal Sovereign* is seen at the head of a Cambridge buffet express. These trains were known irreverently to the undergraduates of the University as 'Beer Trains'. There appears to be little sign of movement, smoke or steam so it is just possible that this was a posed photograph. Nonetheless, it serves well to illustrate Thompson's 'B2' design. Under British Railways, the engine became No. 61671 and remained as the royal engine until No. 70000 *Britannia* arrived. (C. K. L. Coles)

Below: Although Thomas Worsdell intended his Class Y14 0-6-0 principally as a freight engine, in LNER days as 'J15s' they were often seen on passenger duties and they came to make the Felixstowe branch their own. In August 1931 No. 7641 is seen departing Felixstowe Beach with a rake of six-wheeled coaches. (Author's collection)

It is September 1938 and Sentinel Class Y1/1 0-4-0T No. 8400 is pictured shunting at Lowestoft sea wall. These locomotives were built to negotiate tight radii found in docks and other constricted areas. This locomotive was the first Sentinel to be acquired by the LNER and entered service in September 1925 for departmental duties at Lowestoft Harbour. It was renumbered 7772 in April 1943 and again 8130 as part of the 1946 renumbering scheme. Allocated No. 68130 at Nationalisation, by the early 1950s the locomotive had become No. 37 in the departmental series. It was withdrawn in January 1956. (C. S. Perrier Collection/ Colour-Rail (NE96))

Above: At Bishop's Stortford in 1938 Belpaire-boilered Class D15 4-4-0 No. 8891 gleams in ex-works condition LNER lined black livery. The 'D15s' weighed 52 ton 4 cwt. It is coupled to a round-topped tender originally used for oil burning. Built as GER No. 1891 in April 1900 and becoming LNER No. 8891 in 1923, by the date of this photograph the locomotive had been fitted with a GN-pattern chimney. Renumbered 2502 in 1946 and 62502 at Nationalisation, the 'D15' was to remain in service until February 1952. (The Pendragon Collection/Colour-Rail (NE125))

Below: That unpleasant affair with the little Austrian Corporal is but a few months past and War Department 2-10-0 No. 73783 has yet to be demobbed for it was still in khaki livery and bearing the 8th Army Crest when photographed on March shed in October 1945. A total of 150 of these Austerity 2-10-0s were built by the North British Locomotive Co. in 1943–45; this particular example was constructed as part of the last batch of fifty in 1945 and was thus relatively new when photographed here. When transferred to BR ownership, the locomotive was renumbered 90759. (The late H. N. James/Colour-Rail (WD4))

Above: In August 1937 Class 3P 4-4-2T No. 2154 rests on Plaistow shed in lined LMS black. This locomotive was one of a batch of locomotives built by the LMSR at Derby Works – in this case during February 1930 – for use on the ex-LT&SR lines. By January 1948, when it was renumbered 41972 by BR, the locomotive had been reallocated far away from its traditional haunts, being one of the quartet of the class transferred to Dundee. However, the locomotives proved less than suitable for their new duties and were quickly transferred again southwards. Nominally reallocated to Skipton, the locomotives in fact spent the rest of their careers in store at Durran Hill (Carlisle) before, in No. 41972's case, official withdrawal in February 1955. (L. Hanson/Colour-Rail (LM41))

Below: In order to augment the Stanier tanks, which had been introduced on the LT&SR lines in 1934 (and one of which, No. 2500, is now preserved as part of the National Collection at York), some Riddles-designed BR Standard Class 4MT 2-6-4Ts were brought into use on the system. In April 1959 No. 80133 passes Plaistow with an Up Tilbury line service. (T. B. Owen/Colour-Rail (BRM530))

Above: Ex-LT&SR Class 3F 0-6-2T No. 41986 is pictured in steam at Plaistow shed. This class of engine could be forgiven if it had suffered from an identity crisis for all of them carried five different numbers during their lives. They were built by North British Locomotive in two batches in 1913 and 1908. No. 41986 (Works No. 185041) started life as LT&SR No. 75 *Canvey Island*. When taken over by the Midland Railway, it was renumbered 2186 and at the Grouping became 2226. In 1939 it reverted to its original Midland Railway number, then in 1947 was again renumbered, becoming No. 1986 and finally No. 41986 under British Railways. As such the locomotive was withdrawn in February 1959. (W Potter/Colour-Rail (BRM543))

Below: The 'Tilbury Universal Machines' were long-lived. The LMS classified them '3P' and built them long after the LT&SR had ceased to exist. No. 41978, seen here in March 1956 on Shoeburyness shed, was built by the LMS in 1930 and was the last one to be constructed. (T. B. Owen/Colour-Rail (BRM699))

This book is, perhaps, not the place for preservation but this picture is too good to miss for it shows the full glory of the London, Tilbury & Southend Railway passenger locomotive livery. In March 1956 the preserved 'Tilbury Universal Machine' No. 80 *Thundersley* was photographed at Westcliff-on-Sea with a Railway Correspondence & Travel Society special. The locomotive is now to be seen at Bressingham Steam Museum near Diss in Norfolk. It was originally named *Southend-on-Sea* when built by Robert Stephenson & Co. (Works No. 3367) in 1909. It became MR No. 2177, a number which it retained until renumbering in October 1929 when it became No. 2148. On Nationalisation it became No. 41966, an identity it retained until restored to LT&SR livery. *Thundersley* was withdrawn in June 1956 when it was the last of the LT&SR-built 4-4-2Ts remaining. (J. B. McCann/Colour-Rail (R285))

Passing Bentley crossing whilst climbing Beccles Bank, Class B17/6 No. 61622 *Alnwick Castle* is pictured at the head of the 6.18 p.m. Yarmouth–Liverpool Street service. The rake consists of Gresley stock in 'blood and custard' in August 1957. (E. Alger/Colour-Rail (BRE554))

Above: Class B17/6 No. 61664 *Liverpool* puts up a fine exhaust leaving Yarmouth with the 3.14 p.m. service for Liverpool Street in April 1957. The stock appears to be British Railways Mk 1s. It always seemed somewhat incongruous to see locomotives in East Anglia named after football clubs that had their grounds miles from the area in which they were operating. It defies comprehension just why the directors of the LNER failed to name just one of the 'B17s' after an East Anglian football club – there were, after all, sufficient from which to choose. (E. Alger/Colour-Rail (BRE559))

Below: Class J69 0-6-0T No. 68549 is dwarfed beside BR Standard Pacific No. 70001 *Lord Hurcomb* on Stratford shed in February 1962, when the former was coming to the end of its long operational life. Built in May 1894 as GER No. 373, the locomotive was converted to 'J69' configuration in November 1906. Becoming No. 7373 in 1923 and then No. 8549 in 1946, the locomotive was to be withdrawn as BR No. 68549 in February 1962. The 'Britannia' Pacific was built in February 1951 and allocated to the Eastern Region from new, initially at Stratford. No. 70001 was eventually to be transferred to the London Midland Region, from where it was withdrawn in September 1966. (T. A. Murphy/Colour-Rail (UKE937))

In May 1958 ex-GER Class J15 0-6-0 No. 65456 crosses the timber trestle bridge at Wickham Bishops on the Maldon branch with the 3.5 p.m. service from Maldon to Witham. Fittingly the leading vehicle of the pair is a Great Eastern Railway composite in brown. By this date, the 'J15' was entering the last few months of its life; it was withdrawn in September of the same year. Built at Stratford in June 1906 as GER No. 558, the locomotive became No. 7558 at the Grouping, being subsequently renumbered 5456 in the LNER's 1946 renumbering scheme. (C. Hogg/Colour-Rail (BRE1216))

Colour shots from the lesser-known East Anglian lines are none too plentiful which makes this picture of Class B17/6 No. 61666 *Nottingham Forest* all the more welcome. This three-coach local train is on the single track near Glemsford with the 2.2 p.m. local service from Colchester to Cambridge in June 1959. To reach this point, the train would have left Colchester heading in the Up direction and branched off the main line at Witham, then taken the westbound line from Long Melford. From here it will run through Haverhill, Bartlow and Shelford to gain the Varsity City. (G. H. Hunt/Colour-Rail (BRE1342))

In September 1958, Class B17/6 No. 61656 *Leeds United* leaves St Olaves, which is the first station north of Haddiscoe on the line towards Yarmouth, with an Up local. The locomotive carries the second BR emblem on its tender and hauls a rake of coaches in a mixture of liveries behind it. (E. Alger/Colour-Rail (BRE1388))

An immaculate Class K3 Mogul No. 61953 passes Oulton's Up distant signal in the wide sandy cutting where the 6 ft way was rather more than 6 ft. The train is an Up Saturday extra express from Lowestoft in September 1958. (E. Alger/Colour-Rail (BRE1401))

Above: Ex-LNER Class K3 Mogul No. 61957, pictured in near ex-works condition, leaves Lowestoft with an Up 'Holiday Camps Express'. Whilst the locomotive carries no headboard, the rake of beautifully clean Gresley coaches are adorned with roofboards. (E. Alger/Colour-Rail (BRE1402))

Below: Class L1 2-6-4T No. 67704 is pictured at Hopton-on-Sea, located between Yarmouth and Lowestoft on the Norfolk & Suffolk Joint line, with a Holiday Camp special in June 1957. Note two Camping Coaches mounted on the platform. In the days before there was the level of car ownership that is known today, the railways carried most people to their annual fortnight by the sea and the Camping Coaches situated throughout the country were extremely popular. No. 67704 was the fourth of the class to be built – at Darlington (Works No. 2022) in February 1948 – and was originally allocated No. 9003 in the LNER list. The first fifteen of the type were numbered in the 9xxx sequence before it became evident that many of that number range were already allocated. As a result, the 'L1s' were renumbered 67701 et seq, with No. 9003 becoming No. 67704. At the date of this photograph, No. 67704 was allocated to Lowestoft; it was to be withdrawn from Stratford in November 1960. (E. Alger/Colour-Rail (BRE1403))

Above: In May 1959 Class 7MT Pacific No. 70011 *Hotspur* was caught in St Olaves cutting with a Down Yarmouth express. Built in May 1951, No. 70011 was allocated to Norwich when new and was still based there in early 1959. By July 1962, the locomotive had migrated to March. *Hotspur* was to be withdrawn from Carlisle Kingmoor shed in December 1967. (E. Alger/Colour-Rail (BRE1414))

Below: Happy days! Such a sight will never be seen again. This is Melton Constable shed in 1958 and facing the camera are Class J67/2 0-6-0T No. 68536 and Class D16/3 4-4-0 No. 62561 whilst three Ivatt Moguls have their tenders to the camera together with a 'J17' 0-6-0. The 'J60' was built as GER No. 359 as a Class R24 (LNER Class J67) in April 1892. It was rebuilt to 'J69' in June 1904 and was renumbered 7359 at the Grouping. A further rebuild, with a 160-psi boiler, in September 1939 saw the locomotive redesignated Class J67/2. In this form (and having been renumbered 8536 in 1946 and 68536 in 1948), the locomotive was to remain in service until February 1958. Thus when recorded here the 0-6-0T was coming to the end of its sixty-six-year life. (Bruce Chapman Collection/Colour-Rail (BRE955))

Above: The 'Claud Hamilton' 4-4-0s received lined black livery under British Railways but, as time passed, the lining was often forgotten when they passed through works. From 1956 comes this photograph of 'D16/3' No. 62561 looking reasonably clean on Melton Constable shed still with the first British Railways crest upon the tender. Built as GER No. 1830 in March 1908, the locomotive became No. 8830 at the Grouping. Originally constructed as a Class D15, No. 8830 was rebuilt as a 'D16/3' in March 1940. The locomotive was withdrawn from service in February 1958. (Bruce Chapman Collection/Colour-Rail (BRE1127))

Below: Dating from 1956, and possibly on the same day at Melton Constable shed, Class 117 (GER Class G58) 0-6-0 No. 65586 basks in the sunshine. It is gratifying to note, this far from the event, that photographers had the foresight to capture the mundane as well as the glamorous locomotives in colour. A total of forty-four Class J17s were built for the GER along with forty-six Class J16s. The latter were, by January 1932, all rebuilt, in the '117' form. No. 63586, built as GER No. 1236 in December 1910 and becoming No. 8236 at Grouping, was one of the original 'J17' designs. This particular locomotive was to be one of the longest lasting of the type, being withdrawn in April 1962. (Bruce Chapman Collection/Colour-Rail (BKE1350))

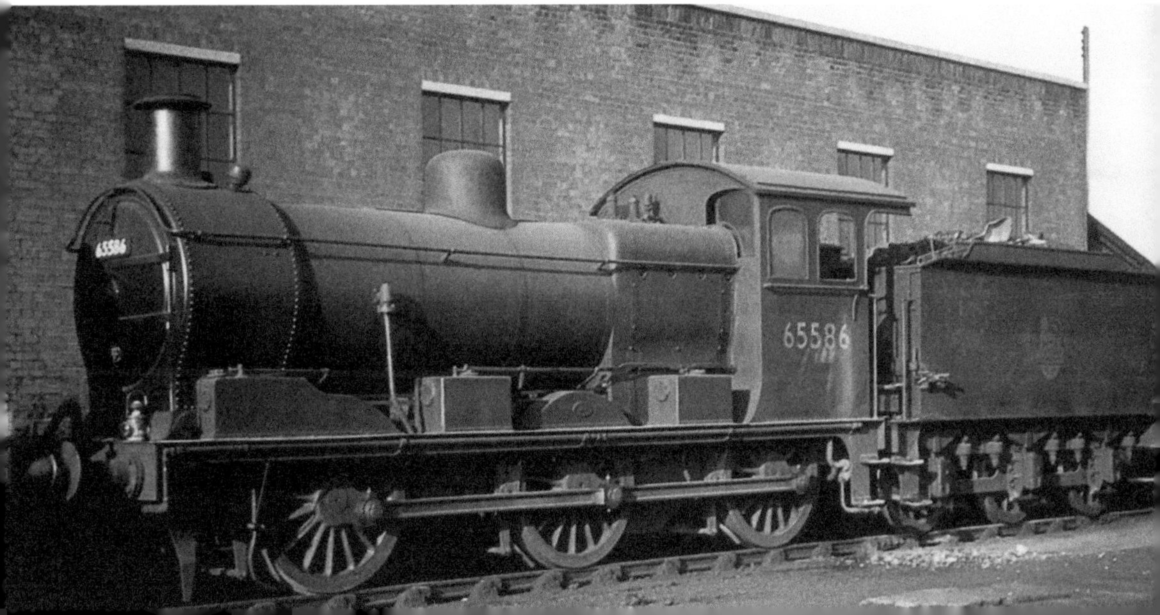

Above: Some thirty-five years after the end of the Great Eastern Railway as an independent concern it was still possible to find traces of the long-disappeared company. This sign, warning against trespass on the railway, was photographed at Witham on 3 May 1958. (K. L. Cook/Rail Archive Stephenson)

Below: It is February 1959 and the last day of the Midland & Great Northern Joint Railway. One of Alfred Hill's Class N7/2 0-6-2Ts No. 69698 finds itself at King's Lynn, far from its birthplace at Stratford, with the connection from South Lynn. The locomotive wears full lined black livery and bears the original British Railways crest. What wanton vandalism to abandon a complete railway system. (R. Reed/Colour-Rail (BRE1406))

Above: On 10 May 1958 Class J69/2 No. 68513 is pictured with the Maldon branch goods near Witham. Built as one of Holden's GBR Class R24 – later LNER Class J67 – in November 1890, No. 401 became LNER No. 7401 at the Grouping and No. 8513 under the LNER's renumbering scheme of 1946. The locomotive was rebuilt to 'J69/2' form – with a higher boiler pressure – in June 1952, the penultimate locomotive to be so treated. Withdrawal was to come in October 1960. The branch to Maldon from Witham opened in 1848. Passenger services over the route ceased in September 1964 and freight was withdrawn in April 1966. (K. L. Cook/Rail Archive Stephenson)

Below: Looking superb in lined Brunswick green livery, Class B17/6 'Sandringham' No. 61652 *Darlington* departs from Cambridge on 22 June 1958 with an Up slow service towards Liverpool Street. Built in April 1936 at, appropriately, Darlington Works and originally numbered 2852, this particular locomotive was rebuilt to 'B17/6' condition in March 1948. As such, the locomotive was to remain in service until September 1959. (K. L. Cook/Rail Archive Stephenson)

Marks Tey, on the Chelmsford–Colchester section of the ex-GER main line, is the junction for the line to Sudbury. Originally the branch headed north from Sudbury to Long Melford, where it divided with lines heading towards Cambridge and towards Bury St Edmunds. At Chappel & Wakes Colne station an alternative route, the Colne Valley Railway, headed westwards towards Cambridge via Haverhill. On 27 September 1958, Ivatt '4MT' 2-6-0 No. 46469 enters Marks Tey station with the 12.1 p.m. service to Haverhill via the Colne Valley line. The line from Marks Tey to Sudbury – the only section of the line still open – first saw services in July 1849. The independent Colne Valley & Halstead Railway opened from Chappel & Wakes Colne to Halstead in April 1860 and thence to Haverhill in May 1863. Passenger trains ceased to use the Colne Valley line in December 1961 and freight ceased in April 1965. (K. L. Cook/Rail Archive Stephenson)

Pictured at Bethnal Green on 11 October 1958 with the 10.32 a.m. service from Liverpool Street to Enfield Town is 'N7' class 0-6-2T No. 69660. This locomotive was one of a batch of twenty built by Robert Stephenson & Co. between October 1925 and January 1926. Originally numbered 941 by the LNER, No. 69660 emerged in November 1925 (Works No. 3905) and was rebuilt with a round-top firebox in September 1943, the first of the Stephenson-built examples to be so treated. Renumbered 9660 in 1946, the locomotive was to survive in service until May 1959, shortly after the date of this photograph. (K. L. Cook/Rail Archive Stephenson)

Opposite below: On 27 September 1958, Class E4 2-4-0 No. 62785 heads a Railway Club brake van special near Inworth on the line from Kelvedon to Tollesbury. Worked by the GER from the start, the Kelvedon, Tiptree & Tollesbury Pier Light Railway was opened in two stages: from Kelvedon, where it formed a junction with the GER main line, to Tollesbury on 1 October 1904 and thence to Tollesbury Pier on 15 May 1907. By the date of this photograph, passenger services had already ceased over the line, being withdrawn on 7 May 1951. Freight services were to continue from Kelvedon to Tiptree until 1 October 1962. Designed by Holden and introduced in 1891, by the date of this photograph the 'E4' class was reduced to this single example which was to be a popular choice for enthusiast excursions from its home shed at Cambridge. Following withdrawal, No. 62785, the last example of a 2-4-0 in service, was to be preserved as part of the National Collection. (K. L. Cook/Rail Archive Stephenson)

A wonderful period shot, dating from 1 November 1958, of the approaches to Liverpool Street station. To the left is the ex-North London Railway station at Broad Street – which has now been subsumed into the massive Broadgate redevelopment – whilst on the right is the Great Eastern Hotel. One of the great railway hotels, the Great Eastern first opened in 1884 and was extended in the early years of the twentieth century. The GER's terminus at Liverpool Street opened for suburban services on 2 February 1874 with the remainder of the station opening on 1 November 1875, when the original terminus at Bishopsgate was to close. The original station design was the work of the GER's Engineer, Edward Wilson, although this was significantly extended in the 1890s. The view illustrated here is as historic as the fashions portrayed; the buildings illustrated here were swept away in the redevelopment of Liverpool Street station, work which saw the extension of the train site towards the photographer and the construction of a new station entrance. (K. L. Cook/Rail Archive Stephenson)

Above: On 1 November 1958 Class B1 No. 61287 passes Hackney Downs with the Up 11.10 a.m. service from Cambridge to London Liverpool Street. This particular locomotive was constructed by the North British Locomotive Co. (Works No. 26188) in February 1948 and was to survive in service until September 1962.

Below: Stratford (30A)-allocated Class N7/5 0-6-2T No. 69645 passes Clapton Sidings on 4 April 1959 with the 10.25 a.m. service from Chingford to Liverpool Street. The first of Hill's 'L77' class was introduced in 1915 but only twelve had been built by the demise of the GER at Grouping; subsequently, a further 122 were built by the LNER, with production ceasing in December 1928. No. 69645 was one of a batch built at Gorton, being constructed in September 1926. Originally numbered 853 and classified 'N7/1', the locomotive became No. 9645 in the LNER renumbering of 1946. The locomotive was reclassified as 'N7/5' in May 1955 when a round-top firebox was fitted; No. 69645 was one of the last of the type to be so treated. Withdrawal came in September 1962 when all the surviving members of the class were taken out of service. In GER days, the improved suburban services to Chingford and Enfield were known by the nickname of 'The Jazz', as a result of the coloured bands used on the coaches to identify the various classes. (K. L. Cook/ Rail Archive Stephenson)

Above: Another 0-6-2T, this time 'N7/3' No. 69721, is pictured on a suburban service, the 1.42 p.m. from Liverpool Street to Enfield Town. Built in June 1928 at Doncaster (Works No. 1688), the locomotive was originally numbered 2619. The 'N7/3s', introduced in November 1927, were the first of the type to be fitted with the round-top firebox from new. A total of thirty-two of this sub-class were built between November 1927 and December 1928. No. 69721 was one of a number to be withdrawn from service in September 1961. (K. L. Cook/Rail Archive Stephenson)

Below: Looking pristine in ex-works condition, Class B1 4-6-0 No. 61223 stands outside the shed at Stratford on 5 April 1930. The gleaming paintwork makes a striking contrast with the careworn locomotive in the background. Constructed by North British (Works No. 26124) in August, at this time the locomotive was allocated to Norwich (32A) shed. Withdrawal was to come in January 1966. (K. L. Cook/Rail Archive Stephenson)

It is now easy to forget that the railways once operated large numbers of summer specials to and from the numerous holiday camps that were established around the coast. These camps were an integral part in the creation of the traditional summer holiday and introduced the seaside to countless thousands. On 5 September 1959, Class B1 No. 61363 heads a Down Butlins Holiday Camp special to the south of Colchester. (K. L. Cook/Rail Archive Stephenson)

During the late 1950s, a number of locomotives were maintained in superb external condition at Stratford for use as station pilots at Liverpool Street. The two locomotives selected were 'N7' No. 69614 and 'J69/1' No. 68619. Pictured outside Stratford shed on 7 June 1959 is No. 69713, the locomotive is in superb external condition. At the time, No. 69713 was allocated to Bishops Stortford. It was built at Doncaster Works in January 1928 as No. 2611. The locomotive was renumbered 9713 in 1946. Despite the locomotive's appearance, however, No. 69713 was coming towards the end of its operational career, being withdrawn in September 1961. (K. L. Cook/Rail Archive Stephenson)

With Nationalisation, there was an increasing likelihood that locomotives previously alien to the lines in East Anglia would be seen. A number of the Ivatt-designed Class 4MT Moguls, introduced in 1947, were allocated to Eastern Region sheds, most notably to Colchester and Norwich, by the late 1950s. One of those allocated to Colchester, No. 43153, heads the 12.10 p.m. service from Clacton to Sheffield south of Colchester on 5 September 1959. (K. L. Cook/Rail Archive Stephenson)

Above: On 5 September 1959, Class B17/6 No. 61670 *City of London* heads towards London with the Up 11.20 a.m. service from Yarmouth South Town to Liverpool Street. The train is pictured just south of Colchester. Originally numbered 2870 by the LNER, the locomotive was one of a batch of eleven built by Robert Stephenson & Co. in 1937 (Works No. 4132). It was one of two – the other being No. 2859 *East Anglian* – to be given 'A4'-style streamlining for use on the 'East Anglian' service between Liverpool Street and Norwich. The streamlined locomotives were launched on the service in September 1937. The two locomotives were to retain their streamline appearance until 1951 (and were classified 'B17/5' during that period), although modifications – such as the removal of the valances over the motion – were undertaken during World War 2. With the removal of the streamlining, the two locomotives were rebuilt to 'B17/6' specification with Thompson boilers pressed to 225 psi. No. 61670 was withdrawn in April 1960. The locomotive was originally named *Manchester City* in May 1937, before being renamed *Tottenham Hotspur* later the same month and subsequently *City of London* in September 1937. (K. L. Cook/Rail Archive Stephenson)

Below: For many years the BR Standard 'Britannia' class Pacifics became synonymous with main line services over the ex-Great Eastern main line from Liverpool Street to Norwich. On this occasion No. 70036 *Boadicea* is pictured heading south from Colchester with the 3.8 p.m. service from Norwich to Liverpool Street. The date is 5 September 1959. No. 70036 was built originally in December 1952, the locomotive being initially allocated to Stratford shed. By July 1962, No. 70036 was allocated to Immingham. Along with the rest of the class, it ended its career allocated to the London Midland Region, being withdrawn in October 1966. (K. L. Cook/Rail Archive Stephenson)

Above: Caught in the early autumn sun on 3 October 1959 – a year characterised by one of the best postwar summers – 'Britannia' class Pacific No. 70010 *Owen Glendower* makes a fine sight as it heads southbound near Chelmsford with the 2 p.m. service from Clacton to Liverpool Street. Built in May 1951, No. 70010 was initially allocated to Norwich shed when new for operation over the ex-GER main line to London. As with the majority of the class, the locomotive was to be withdrawn ultimately from Carlisle Kingmoor shed, succumbing in September 1967. (K. L. Cook/Rail Archive Stephenson)

Below: By the start of the 1960s, the steam-hauled suburban services into Liverpool Street station were reaching the end. On 28 August 1961 Class L1 2-6-4T No. 67735 was the motive power for the North Woolwich–Stratford (Low Level) service. The train is pictured at Thames Wharf Junction. The 'L1' design was one of the few classes to emerge from the LNER during Edward Thompson's relatively short period at the helm. Appointed following the death of Sir Nigel Gresley in 1941, Thompson was CME of the LNER from then until his retirement on 30 June 1946. Inevitably his period of control was dominated by the exigencies of World War 2 and he is, perhaps, best known as the designer of the 'B1' 4-6-0. The first of his 'L1' class 2-6-4Ts emerged in May 1945 and ultimately 100 were built. No. 67735 was constructed by the North British Locomotive Co. (as Works No. 26574) in November 1948 and was throughout its career a Stratford-allocated locomotive. It was withdrawn from the London shed, shortly after the date of this photograph, in September 1962. (K. L. Cook/Rail Archive Stephenson)

Above: During the spring of 1959, Class B17/6 No. 61641 *Gayton Hall* is captured departing from March. At this stage, the locomotive was not far from home, being allocated to March (31B) shed. This particular locomotive was constructed as No. 2841 at Darling Works in May 1933. Rebuilt as a 'B17/6' in February 1949, the locomotive was to survive until January 1960. (Derek Penney)

Below: Another Class B17/6, this time No. 61618 *Wynyard Park*, receives attention at Cambridge (31A) shed in early 1959. At this time the locomotive was allocated to Ipswich (32B). Again a product of Darlington Works, this time in November 1930, and originally numbered 2818, No. 61618 was rebuilt into a 'B17/6' during April 1958, the last locomotive to be so treated. Its career as a 'B17/6' was, however, to be of relatively short duration, as No. 61618 was withdrawn less than two years later in January 1960. (Derek Penney)

Above: Class B1 4-6-0 No. 61200 is caught south of Cambridge at the head of a southbound express passenger working towards London in early 1959. At this time the locomotive was allocated to King's Cross (34A) shed. Built by North British (Works No. 26101) in June 1947, No. 61200 was one of the 'B1s' to succumb in December 1962; that year was the first in which significant numbers of the class were withdrawn, as steam was gradually eliminated from Eastern Region metals. (Derek Penney)

Below: Pictured on March (31B) shed during the winter of 1958/59, Class D16/3 No. 62589 was already approaching the end of its near fifty-year life. Built as GER No. 1819 in June 1910, the locomotive became No. 8819 at Grouping and No. 2589 under the LNER's 1946 renumbering scheme. Converted to 'D16/3' format in March 1947, No. 62589 was to be withdrawn in May 1959. (Derek Penney)

Above: Two Class B17/6s, No. 61627 *Aske Hall* and No. 61620 *Clumber*, are seen on shed at March during the winter of 1958/59. At this date the former was allocated to March and the latter to King's Lynn (31C). No. 61620 was built at Darlington in November 1930 as LNER No. 2820 and was rebuilt as a 'B17/6' in December 1951. No. 61627 was also a product of Darlington, as LNER No. 2827 in March 1931. This locomotive was converted to 'B17/6' slightly earlier, in November 1948. The locomotives were withdrawn in July 1959 (No. 61627) and January 1960 (No. 61620). (Derek Penney)

Below: Class E4 2-4-0 No. 62785 is pictured at Mildenhall during the summer of 1958. Allocated in its later years to Cambridge shed and a familiar sight on the ex-GER lines that ran east from Cambridge to Mildenhall and towards Haverhill, No. 62785 was the last locomotive with this wheel arrangement to operate on BR. Built as a representative of Holden's 'T26' class, the locomotive was one of 100 built between 1891 and 1902, All of the class passed to the LNER in 1923, but withdrawals meant that only eighteen survived into BR ownership. Always a popular locomotive for use on specials in its latter days, No. 62785 was to be preserved as part of the National Collection on withdrawal in December 1959. (Derek Penney)

Above: No. 62785 is seen again, this time at the head of a train in Mildenhall station itself in the summer of 1958. The Mildenhall branch opened in two stages: from Cambridge to Fordham, on the Newmarket–Ely line, on 2 June 1884 and thence to the terminus at Mildenhall on 1 April 1885. The Mildenhall branch was not to outlive the 'E4' by long, with passenger services being withdrawn on 18 June 1962 and freight on 15 July 1964. The station buildings still survive, having been rebuilt into a substantial private house. (Derek Penney)

Below: During the summer of 1958 Class B12 No. 61516 departs King's Lynn. This particular locomotive was built in November 1913 as GER No. 1516. It became LNER No. 8516 at Grouping and then reverted to its original GER number in the LNER renumbering scheme of 1946. It was converted to 'B12/3' form in November 1932, one of the first to be so treated, and was also the first of the class to be fitted with the Lentz poppet valve gear in place of the normal Stephenson link motion (in December 1926). This latter modification was to last until November 1932. By the date of this photograph, No. 61516 was already on borrowed time; the locomotive was withdrawn at the end of July 1958. (Derek Penney)

Above: Class J17 0-6-0 No. 65554 is pictured on March shed on a summer's day in the late 1950s. Built as GER No. 1204 in December 1902, this locomotive was rebuilt converted from 'J16' to 'J17' in January 1923 as one of the first to be treated by the LNER in continuation of the earlier GER policy. Becoming No. 8204 at Grouping and then No. 5554 in 1946, the locomotive was to be withdrawn in September 1961. (Derek Penney)

Below: Captured in the summer sun in lined green livery towards the end of its operational career, Class B17/1 No. 61643 *Champion Lodge* still looks in fine condition as it awaits its next duty at March station. This particular example of the class was built at Darlington in May 1935 as LNER No. 2853. Conversion to 'B17/6' came in October 1954, one of the last to be so treated, and withdrawal in July 1958. (Derek Penney)

Above: Cambridge was the easternmost point reached by the metals of the erstwhile London & North Western Railway – courtesy of the line from Bletchley and Sandy – and thus residents of the area would have been familiar with ex-LNWR locomotives. Pictured, however, slightly away from ex-LNWR metals at March shed in April 1958 is ex-LNWR Class 7F No. 49115. (Derek Penney)

Below: Looking in excellent external condition in its lined green livery, Class B17/6 No. 61626 *Brancepeth Castle* stands near to the coaling stage at March shed in April 1958. (Derek Penney)

The Final Act

With the cessation of hostilities in 1945 it was clear that a General Election would not be far away. Given the state of the economy after six years of total war there was little that divided the two main political parties in the United Kingdom on policy, least of all that the railways would have to be taken under state control – the only divergence of opinion was the manner in which it should be done.

As history relates, the Labour Party under Clement Attlee won a landslide victory and the railways of mainland Britain, with the exception of some narrow gauge lines, were taken into state ownership from midnight on 31 December 1947.

With the knowledge that the legislation would be passed, from mid-1947 plans were put in hand to look into the needs for future traction on the railways: electrification was abandoned as being too expensive at the time and new steam locomotives would be the order of the day. A little over three years after the creation of British Railways the first Standard steam locomotive was named at Marylebone – a remarkable feat by any standards.

Robert Riddles CBE was appointed to the position of Chief Electrical & Mechanical Engineer of the new organisation and it was under his auspices that Stewart Cox created the first Standard Pacific. With the exception of a small number of engines which had appeared in the latter days of the LMSR, its appearance was unlike anything previously seen on the railways of Britain for the driving wheels were totally exposed with the running plate above them in order to ease maintenance.

In all there were just 999 Standard steam engines: the first of them was numbered 70000 and named *Britannia* by the then Minister of Transport, Mr Alfred Barnes, at that ceremony at Marylebone station.

After running in the locomotive was allocated to Stratford where it was joined by the following seven members of the class. The next seven were allocated to Norwich; in theory East Anglia now had fifteen Pacifics at its command but No. 70004 *William Shakespeare* was sent for display at the Festival of Britain exhibition in London in 1951 and, upon release from there, went on more or less permanent loan to the Southern Region where it was joined by No. 70014 *Iron Duke*. No. 70009 *Alfred the Great* also spent some time on the Southern Region.

The Stratford men loved them. They were the first Pacifics to be allocated specifically to the Great Eastern Section and the crews had never had such power at their command. The schedule from the capital to Ipswich was brought down to an hour and a quarter and it look forty years and the coming of electrification to reduce that time to the even hour.

The 'Britannias' were made responsible for all the major expresses in East Anglia and they held sway until the first of the main line diesels was drafted in, but the new motive power could not better the times achieved by the last steam engines.

East Anglia was the first area of England to be purged of steam traction. In the very early 1960s the remaining working engines were drafted away to work out the remainder of their lives on other regions and that most evocative of machines yet devised by man was to be seen.

Class N7 0-6-2T No. 9707 stands on Norwich shed turntable on 4 March 1950. Two years after Nationalisation, the locomotive still wears its London & North Eastern Railway identity. The 'N7s' saw service throughout East Anglia but had been principally intended for use on the intensive commuter services in the London suburbs. The first two members of the class were delivered in January and February 1915, but No. 1002 did not appear for a further six years: they were then built continuously by the Great Eastern and the LNER until 1928. Apart from Stratford, various makers were employed: the first twenty-two were constructed at Stratford, followed by a batch of thirty from Gorton. There then came twenty-one from Robert Stephenson & Co., followed by another ten from Gorton. W. Beardmore & Co. provided the next twenty and the final thirty-two came from Doncaster. This particular example was built at Doncaster in November 1927 and was withdrawn in April 1961. (K. Harrison)

Above: On 23 July 1949, No. 61670 is seen running on to the turntable at Norwich shed. The livery appears to be black and there is no evidence of lining and, judging by the amount of coal in the tender, a trip to London cannot be far away. It is quite likely that this engine did not receive Brunswick green livery until alter the streamlining was removed. (K. Harrison)

Below: The 'Fenman' was a titled train instituted by BR in 1949 but by no stretch of the imagination could it be described as a star turn. The main portion of the train started from Hunstanton with the buffet car at 6.45 a.m., calling at all stations over the 15.25 miles to King's Lynn where it arrived at 7.21 a.m., reversed and departed at 7.30 a.m. With stops at Downham and Ely; it strolled at a leisurely pace across the Fenlands to make its appearance at Cambridge sixty-one minutes later. A portion of the train had left Bury St Edmunds at 7.57 a.m. and, running through Newmarket, it meandered into the Varsity City ten minutes after the main section. Without too much urgency, the train was assembled and departed at 8.48 a.m. for London where it eventually materialised at 10.3 a.m., the journey of 112.25 miles taking no less than three hours eighteen minutes. The Down journey took three hours twenty-five minutes, representing an average speed of just 33 mph. Moreover, the powers that be had the effrontery to dignify the train with express headcoding as witnessed by this picture of 'Claud Hamilton' 4-4-0 No. 2614 at its head. Whilst the precise date is not known, it must have been early in the train's life for the locomotive is still in LNER apple green livery with the number painted on the buffer beam. (Author's collection)

This was a sight not often seen: a WD Austerity 2-8-0 on a passenger working. But all is not as it seems, for No. 90042 was working a fourteen-carriage empty coaching stock train near Cambridge on 4 August 1953. The stock was a motley collection. This locomotive was originally WD No. 77437 and was built by the North British Locomotive Co. in 1944. This was one of 200 of the type acquired by the LNER, Nos 3000–3199, in February 1947, being classified '07'. This particular locomotive was numbered 3042 by the LNER. (R. Harrison)

Before the coining of the Standard Pacifics, the Great Eastern section of the Eastern Region was suffering a severe motive power shortage and to alleviate the situation some ex-Southern Railway Light Pacifics were drafted in on loan. Notwithstanding the fact that the 'Britannia' Pacifics came on stream early in 1951, the Bulleid engines were still working in East Anglia in the November of that year. On the 3rd of that month, 'Battle of Britain' Pacific No. 34065 *Hurricane* is seen leaving Norwich with an express for Liverpool Street. (R. Harrison)

And then they came. In all their glory they came, bringing a breath of fresh air to the East Anglian timetables and proceeded to transform the schedules. The 'Britannia' Pacifics brought power to the Eastern Counties, some areas of which had never been seen such power before. They worked all the expresses between Norfolk and London but on occasion were not too heavily laden as in this picture of No. 70000 *Britannia* herself. The first Standard Pacific was caught on Saturday 13 September 1958 passing Hethersett with the 2.42 p.m. Norwich–Liverpool Street service. Despite the headcode, four coaches could hardly be called a wearisome load for a Class 7 locomotive. Note the Stratford (30A) shedcode. (R. Harrison)

On 4 April 1959 Lowestoft-based Gresley Class K3/2 Mogul No. 61970 passes Norwich Trowse swing bridge with a mixed freight. The locomotive cannot long have been out of works after an overhaul judging by its condition. Introduced in 1924, the 'K3/2' was a development of Gresley's three-cylinder GNR design but built to LNER loading gauge. (R. Harrison)

Class B17/4 4-6-0 No. 61666 *Nottingham Forest* heads a Down Clacton express near Shenfield on 8 July 1954. This engine had been built by Robert Stephenson & Co. (Works No. 4128) and was named in February 1937. This final sub-class of the 'Sandies' were fitted from new with 4,200 gallon 'Group Standard' tenders. Until the coming of the Standard Pacifics, these locomotives, in company with the 'B12s', were responsible for the principal expresses in East Anglia. As the 'Britannias' came on stream the 'old guard' was relegated to the less important expresses. (B Kelley)

The 'E4' 2-4-0 could have been made for the branch lines of Suffolk and Norfolk No. 62789 is seen approaching Barnwell Junction on the Mildenhall branch in 1953. The train consists of an ex-GER coach with steps fitted to the bogie for the use of passengers at halts and another which started life with the North Eastern Railway. This was the 'new set' on the branch. (Author's collection)

On an August afternoon in 1954, Gresley Class K3/3 Mogul No. 61886 starts a semi-fast train for Lowestoft out of Woodbridge. (Author's collection)

LNER Class Y1 0-4-0T No. 7773 reposes on a dockside headshunt at Lowestoft close to the station and the old swing bridge on 3 July 1949. The locomotive is still in full LNER livery. It was destined never to wear its British Railways number, which would have been 68131. The swing bridge referred to is now a modem lifting bridge. (R. Harrison)

Gresley Class B17/2 No. 61627 *Aske Hall* lifts a stopping train for Ely and London out of King's Lynn on Wednesday 25 September 1958. This sub-class was built by the LNER at Darlington and fitted with boilers pressed to 200 psi that had been bought in from Armstrong Whitworth. The locomotive was named in 1931. This locomotive was built as No. 2827 at Darlington Works in March 1931; it was rebuilt as a 'B17/6' in November 1948, being withdrawn in July 1959. (R. Harrison)

Nearly two years after Nationalisation, Class Y3 Sentinel 0-4-0T still carries LNER livery and number 8177 whilst shunting at Lowestoft – probably in the wood yard – but carries some reference to its new owner in the form of 'B. R.(E)'. Its BR number would be 68177. (R. Harrison)

Lowestoft-based Class J15 0-6-0 No. 65462 is seen at Yarmouth Reach shed on 30 July 1949. Eighteen months after Nationalisation the locomotive has acquired its British Railways number but still retains its previous owner's identity upon the tender. The tender is one of those which ran originally with oil-burning locomotives but, obviously, at the time of this photograph had been converted to carry coal. Happily, this locomotive has been preserved and has a home – now coupled to a more conventional tender – on the North Norfolk Railway. It is ironic that one of the few preserved examples of Great Eastern motive power is based upon a railway that was purely Midland & Great Northern Joint. (R. Harrison)

On the morning of 8 July 1954 Class B17/6 4-6-0 No. 61669 *Barnsley* bounds past Shenfield with the Down running of the 'Easterling'. This was the only titled train to run regularly on the East Suffolk main line and the only train not to stop at Ipswich, running nonstop from Liverpool Street to Beccles. At Beccles the train divided, with portions going forward to Lowestoft and Great Yarmouth. The 'Easterling' was introduced by British Railways and ran only in the summer timetable on weekdays. The Class B17/6s were the 'B17/4' modified with the 100A ('B1'-type) boiler. (P. Kelley)

Above: Class B2 4-6-0 No. 61617 *Ford Castle* is pictured on the Liverpool Street turntable turning itself via the vacuum. Originally a 'B17/1', the engine was rebuilt in December 1946 and given a tender from condemned Class C7 4-4-2 No. 706. No. 61617 was the standby royal engine at King's Lynn and it became the locomotive's sad duty in 1952 to convey the body of His Late Majesty King George VI from Wolferton to King's Lynn where the train reversed and No. 70000 *Britannia* took the late King back to his capital. *Ford Castle* had the somewhat doubtful privilege of being the first 'B2' withdrawn. (Author's collection)

Below: 'Britannias' at Ipswich. On a forgotten day in August 1960, No. 70041 *Sir John Moore* enters the station from the tunnel with the Down 12.30 p.m. from Liverpool Street to Norwich whilst the second member of the class, No. 70001 *Lord Hurcomb* takes water awaiting departure for London with an Up Yarmouth express off the East Suffolk main line. By this time there were sufficient Class 7MT Pacifics for them to also be put in charge of the East Suffolk expresses. It is interesting that twelve years after state ownership of the railways, Gresley stock is still in use on express passenger workings for there is one such behind the tender of No. 70001. (Author's collection)

Above: In 1958, Class L1 2-6-4T No. 67706 slows at Felixstowe Town signalbox to pick up the token on a Felixstowe–Ipswich train. The first 'L1' was built at Doncaster in May 1945, but it was not until early 1948 that further examples of the class emerged, this time from Darlington Works. No. 67706 was built at Darlington (Works No. 2024) in February 1948 and was initially numbered E9005. The locomotive was withdrawn from Stratford shed in December 1960. (The late H. N. James)

Below: Standard Class 4MT Mogul No. 76045 was allocated to West Auckland (51F) when it passed the premises of Ransomes, Sims & Jeffries at Ipswich with the 4.36 p.m. Felixstowe Beach–Liverpool Street special on 13 July 1958. (The late H. N. James)

Above: Class B1 4-6-0 No. 61040 *Roedeer* is pictured leaving Norwich with the Up working of the 'East Anglian' at 11.40 a.m. on the last day of May 1951. This engine was the first to be built by the North British Locomotive Co. and the last to be named after a breed of deer. It had a working life of barely more than twenty years, having entered traffic in April 1946 and being withdrawn in July 1966. (LCGB/Ken Nunn Collection)

Below: No. 70003 *John Bunyan* is seen on Trowse Swing Bridge, running light engine from Norwich to Thetford, where it will await the arrival of its train behind the 'J15' No. 65567. (R. Harrison)

On an unknown date, Ivatt LMS-design Class 4MT Mogul No. 43067 approaches Norwich Thorpe with a train of Midland Region stock. The class was introduced in 1947 with taper boiler and double chimney although the single-chimney variant was introduced in 1949. The locomotive was allocated to New England (35A). (R. Harrison)

Above: A 'J17' wearing express passenger headcode is something which one did not see every day but this was something rather special. No. 65587 is seen entering Norwich Thorpe with the last steam working: it was a Railway Correspondence & Travel Society special on 31 March 1962. The train had been brought to Norwich by Class 7MT Pacific No. 70003 *John Bunyan*. (R. Harrison)

Below: British Railways inherited four classes of Pacific tank locomotives from the LNER. All were of North Eastern Railway or Great Central Railway origin and their sorties into East Anglia must have been rare. However, four of them were allocated to Norwich and on Sunday 20 July 1952 Robinson GCR (Class 9N) Class A5 No. 69824 entered Norwich Thorpe from the Lowestoft and Yarmouth direction. (R. Harrison)

Above: On 1 June 1952 Class 7MT Pacific No. 70007 *Coeur de Lion* approached Norwich Thorpe with an express from Liverpool Street when barely a year old, having been constructed in April 1951. The locomotive was allocated to Stratford when new and was based on the Eastern Region for more than a decade before reallocation to the LMR. The locomotive was withdrawn from Carlisle (Kingmoor) in June 1965 and was, therefore, the first of the 'Britannia' class Pacifics to be withdrawn.

Below: The final class of BR Standard locomotives was the '9F' 2-10-0 although the type was never exactly common in East Anglia. Normally the furthest east that they worked was March but the class was known to work down to Stratford. On Saturday 24 October 1964 double-chimney example No. 92191, coupled to a BRIE tender, was found at March.

A stranger far from home on Saturday 3 August 1957: Hughes ex-LMSR 'Crab' Class 5MT Mogul No. 42902 of Burton shed was photographed in the county town of Norfolk. The class gained the nickname 'Crab' because of the strange attenuation of the footplating over the cylinders. The locomotive had arrived via the Wensum Curve (the Norwich avoiding line). It came off its train at Wensum Junction and reversed into Norwich shed light engine before taking a train from Norwich Thorpe station. (R. Harrison)

On Saturday 13 September 1958 Norwich-based (32A) Thompson Class L1 2-6-4T No. 67707 passes Wroxham signal box with a local passenger train. No. 67707 was built at Darlington in February 1948 (Works No. 2025) and was originally numbered E9006 by BR. Based at this time at Norwich, the locomotive was to be allocated subsequently to Colwick before withdrawal from Gorton in July 1961. (R. Harrison)

Above: A little under three years later, on 3 February 1952, Class V3 No. 67679 approaches Thorpe station from Cromer. It wears full BR livery of lined black. Behind the bunker is a Gresley coach in the new livery of carmine and cream, a style which is better known to enthusiasts as 'blood and custard'. (R. Harrison)

Below: There were three titled trains that ran between Norwich and Liverpool Street in BR days: the 'East Anglian' was a name which survived from LNER days, whilst the 'Norfolkman' and the 'Broadsman' were introduced by BR. In Coronation year, 1953, the latter, with specially decorated headboard and supplementary board above the buffer beam, departed from Ipswich on 28 May behind 'Britannia' class Pacific No. 70007 *Coeur de Lion*. (The late H. N. James)

Gresley's glorious 'A4' class Pacific was always a rare sight in East Anglia though the occasional working into Cambridge was not unknown. Due to diversions, on Sunday 29 October 1961 No. 60029 *Woodcock* was photographed between Ely and March with a train of Pullman cars. At the time, the locomotive was allocated to King's Cross (34A – Top Shed). The reversed headboard is tantalising: the 'Harrogate Sunday Pullman', perhaps. (R. Harrison)

The same day saw representatives of all of the LNER's Pacific locomotive designers venturing on to unfamiliar territory. Thompson Class A2/3 was introduced in 1946 as a new construction development of Class A2/2. The latter were the rebuilds of Gresley's earlier 'P2' class 2-8-2s (for which Edward Thompson has yet to be forgiven!). No. 60518 *Tehran* was allocated to York (50A) at the time and was thus a fair distance from home when photographed between Ely and March. (R. Harrison)

The Rural Idyll

East Anglia is a region dominated by agriculture; the many great churches bear testimony to the wealth generated by the wool trade in the Middle Ages and agriculture's importance continued right through the railway age. The result of this was that the area was served by a number of rural branches and small railway companies. These were as much a part of the railway scene as the main line services and epitomised, perhaps, the glory days of the region's railways. The region boasted only one passenger-carrying narrow gauge railway – the Southwold.

The short – two-mile – Eye branch met the Great Eastern main line at Mellis. The line was built by the Mellis & Eye Railway and opened on 1 April 1867. Operated and later absorbed by the Great Eastern Railway, the line was to lose its passenger services on 2 February 1931 and to close completely on 13 July 1964. Here the terminus station at Eye is pictured in 1950. (L&GRP)

One of the independent railways of East Anglia was the Mid-Suffolk Light Railway; although the company had ambitious plans for a network of lines serving the district, in the event only the line from Haughley to Laxfield was opened. Authorised under the Light Railways Act, the line to Laxfield opened on 20 September 1904 to freight traffic and to passenger services nine days later. Shortly after Nationalisation, in April 1949, Class J15 No. 5459 is pictured at Laxfield with a two-coach passenger service. Passenger services to Laxfield ceased on 26 July 1952 and the line closed completely in June 1953. (Ian Allan Library)

The GER possessed a number of branch lines, including that serving Hadleigh. Authorised as the Eastern Union & Hadleigh Railway on 18 June 1846, the 7.5-mile long branch opened formally on 20 August 1847, with actual passenger services starting early the following month. By the date of this photograph – 1949 – passenger services had already ceased, on 29 February 1932, but freight continued until complete closure on 19 April 1965. (L&GRP)

Officially known as the Kelvedon, Tiptree & Tollesbury Pier Light Railway, this line was better known simply as the Kelvedon & Tollesbury. Built under the auspices of the Light Railways Act, the first 8-mile section of the line – from Kelvedon (on the GER main line) to Tollesbury – opened on 1 October 1904 and the remaining 1.5 miles to Tollesbury Pier followed on 15 May 1907. This section was relatively shortlived, closing on 17 July 1921. The line was operated by the GER. Here, in 1950, a two-coach train is pictured at the Low Level station at Kelvedon used by branch services. By this date passenger services were already drawing to a close – they were withdrawn on 7 May 1951 – with the line later closing completely. (L&GPR)

The Wisbech & Upwell was one of the more unusual lines in the region. Constructed as a roadside steam railway, regulations meant that the locomotives – both steam and later diesel – had to have their motion covered.